THE JUDAS FACTOR

CW01494690

BY

MICHAEL.E.ELLAH

"For the wages of sin is death…"
Romans 6:23

"Wash you, make you make you clean; put away the evil of your doings before mine eyes, cease to do evil…But if ye refuse and rebel, ye shall be devoured by the sword; for the mouth of the Lord hath spoken it"
Isaiah 1: 16, 20

'When you betray somebody else, you also betray yourself."
Isaac Bashevis Singer

This book is dedicated to Almighty God for giving me life and the ability to write it twenty-five years ago and also for giving me a second chance at a full life after a severe accident in the intervening years. I thank all my friends and family who encouraged me to write and most particularly my wife Patricia and my daughters; Michelle, Tamar and Patricia ('Ije) who are always and forever in my heart and also implored me not to allow this story to stay unpublished.

M. E. Ellah October 2012.

GLOSSARY

1- 'Ya ya Kasuwa'; Hausa phrase meaning; how's the market
2- 'Oga' ; broken English term for Boss often used as a term of respect
3- 'dey'; broken English term meaning to be in a place or to be doing something
4- 'Say'; broken English term used in place of 'that' in proper English.
5- 'no'; broken English term often used as a substitute for 'don't'
6- 'Wetin'; broken English term used in place of 'what' or 'what is that'.
7- 'Pikin'; broken English word for child.
8- 'Na'; broken English word used as 'is' or 'it's' in the context used in this story.
9- 'Gari'; meal made from cassava, a staple food of the people in many parts of Nigeria and the neighboring countries.
10- 'Eba'; another word for gari.
11- 'Peppersoup'; a clear broth made with fish or meat very popular as an accompaniment to drinking of lager beer, palm wine and other alcoholic beverages.
12- 'Fit'; broken English word used to mean 'can' as in 'can do or not do'.
13- 'Chop'; broken English word meaning 'to eat'.
14- 'Ya nada kyau Hausa phrase meaning; 'he is handsome' or good looking.
15- 'Annoder' broken English word for 'another'.
16- 'Biar' broken English word for 'beer'.
17- 'Congomeat'; slang term for snails
18- 'Betta' : broken English for ' Better'
19- 'Titees'; broken English slang for voluptuous women or girls.
20- 'Quench'; broken English slang for death.
21- 'So tey'; broken English phrase meaning 'until' in the context used in this story.
22- 'Dahling' ; pronounced ' dahleeng' meaning 'darling'
23- 'Dis' ; broken English meaning 'this'

24- 'O'; broken English often used in several contexts as an emphasis of the point being made and as an exclamation.

25- 'Now'; broken English often used differently from the normal English usage meaning presently. It is used to connote encouragement to the action being suggested by the speaker.

26- 'Buredi'; broken English for ' bread'

27- 'Mallams'; Hausa word for itinerant sellers of goods used in the context as a street trader from the North(of Hausa extraction)

28- 'Belle'; broken English meaning 'belly'

29- ''gree'; broken English slang for 'agree'

30- "Egusi"; dried pumpkin seed a special ingredient for making a popular soup often eaten with gari.

31- 'Maroko'; slum shantytown settlement located close to Victoria Island.

32- 'Sabi'; broken English slang word used to mean 'understand' or 'comprehend'.

33- 'knack'; broken English word meaning knock used it the context here to mean 'hit' as in 'knack me one cold beer' ' hit me with a cold beer'

34- 'Chei'; broken English exclamation used to express surprise in the same way as 'wow!'

35- 'Abi'; broken English word used to express the existence of understanding in the context used here the words 'is it that?' can be conveniently substituted for 'abi'.

36- 'wack'; broken English word meaning' to eat'

37- 'Una'; broken English word meaning 'you' for a group of people. Plural' you'

38- 'kai-kai'; locally distilled gin 'moonshine'

39- 'Calabash'; container made from the hard covering of a fruit or vegetable.

40- 'Am'; broken English word for 'it' also used interchangeably with 'him'.

41- 'Commot'; broken English word meaning to 'come out' used to ask a person to leave from one place to the other. It is also used to ask a person to take off something such as a piece of clothing or an item as used in the story.

42- 'Siddon'; broken English word used to instruct or ask a person to 'sit down'

43- 'Haba'; broken English exclamation used to express surprise at a fact or situation.
44- 'Dodo'; slang name for fried plantains a popular inclusion in a meal.   45-   'Aladura'; generic word used to describe religious church group where a white habit is worn as a uniform by all members of the group or church.

PROLOGUE

TARKWA BAY LAGOS; 15th JUNE 1985

Night time: The moon glowed like a silver coin in the clear night air. She ran, stumbling in the sand of the beach as the world swirled about her. She was high on cocaine. She tried to slip off her shoes, her heart raced as she ran through the sand, panting. She was trembling as she heard the sound of the motor-cycle speeding towards her. She turned in frenzy, wide-eyed and afraid, looking for a place to hide as she fell, picked herself up again and continued scurrying towards the large rocks at the curve of the bay. It all seemed dreamlike, as if she were in a trance, soft and slow, each step she took seemed like a leap to her and she fell. It was all real. In fear her stomach felt vacant as though it floated outside her being and she lay there retching and then she vomited on the white sand. He rode her down. As she struggled to stand, he jumped off the motor cycle and held her. It took only a fraction of a second and finally she would be free of him as he held her head in a vice-like grip and snapped her neck with a sharp twist. He let her drop, and without another look from his glazed eyes, he left. The rain came down all at once in large droplets and washed her corpse as the waves broke rhythmically on the beach.

ONE

6.00 P.M- APRIL 16 1985, LAGOS

I

The evening sun glowed orange as the silver Mercedes, gliding smoothly on the asphalt, darted through the city traffic and headed towards Murtala Mohammed International airport at Ikeja. There was, outside of the cool air-conditioned interior of the car, a thick heat that hung over the city. This was Lagos, Africa's largest city, constantly buzzing with life and sweating in the rain forest amid the brackish lakes and lying open to the Atlantic. There was also, in the vast melting pot of human activity, an ever present pursuit of money and power. It made the people vibrant and the city oscillated perpetually.

Mustapha Abdul Rahman and Romano Moreno, his bodyguard, sat in the back of the car listening to Ravel, feigning a visual civility which is often a misleading feature of the nouveau riche. Mustapha sat smoking a cigar filling the car with sweet acrid fumes, it had been a difficult day, every day in the racing city was difficult and he felt beaten, weathered, as he sipped scotch from his silver flask. He was attractive to women only in an animal way as his face was a little too rough-hewn and weathered to be handsome or clean cut. He was a man whose features portrayed power through his strong and prominent jaw line and his skin, tanned to a deep dark brown, was an indication of his outdoor life style and revealed also that the nomadic half-Arab was no stranger to Africa. His features, which were by no means commonplace, did not betray the man who hid behind the mask, but his eyes, placid grey orbs that held the world in contempt, displayed ever so subtly, the cunning and power of the man who had achieved so much and yet so little. It was, more often than not impossible to tell what he was thinking by merely looking at his lazy eyes. It was safe though to assume that he, like an army general, contemplated action, for he was a man of action.

'I'll be back soon, two days at the most... I'm going to say farewell... Ben has to go.' Mustapha said biting on his cigar.

'I never thought much of Ben', Romano said. '...Yesterday the messenger said he had been on the take, nice boy he was sometime...

how did he ever get into such company?' Mustapha replied, his strong African accent still tainted with an Arabic flavor.

'He was always in it sir.' Romano replied.

They were almost at the International Airport, as they drove past the statue of the drumming man towards the ramp. The Challenger 600 was prepared for flight. All the routine checks had been made, the aircraft was stocked with champagne, caviar, king size lobsters and other delicacies. Mustapha boarded the aircraft at a lone gate where Robert Bungham the ex-United States Air force pilot greeted him warmly. A small neatly dressed Immigration Officer stamped one of his many false passports and he was allowed to board. Air traffic control was contacted and the aircraft was cleared to take off. Mustapha took a sleeping pill, knocked it back with a soft drink and slept. Bungham skillfully directed the iron bird into the air as it climbed through the sky past the graying cotton wool clouds, they reached cruising altitude and headed towards London.

II

London, Wednesday 17- 7.00 am

It was cold and wet. A tired looking Mustapha sat in the black Jaguar with two men and a chauffeur. One of them sat quietly, holding a small box in his hands.

'How long is he allowed gaffer?' asked the chauffeur.

'Let him take as long as he wants… I know Lacy and he'll do a good Job' Mustapha said.

They turned into a Kensington Street and parked the car. It was still early and quiet there was hardly much movement in the street. As Mustapha read a magazine, the two men in the car sat nervously twiddling their thumbs.

In the large white flat, a man and woman slept peacefully after an exhausting night of passion. The woman, a small buxom blonde with full lips and an ivory oval face was a fast pickup at a party. The man, Ben a.k.a. *'The Time Piece'* for his shrewd and efficient pickups and payoffs slept deeply, his six foot length sprawled on the circular bed as he dreamt of far off lands, women, tequila and samba. He was far away from his London flat where *light fingered Lacy* had picked the lock and stealthily entered his living room. Lacy opened his little brown bag carefully and as though he were lifting a baby out of a cot he unpacked the nitroglycerine.

Moving around the flat soundlessly, like a cat, he placed the explosives at strategic corners of the room and wired them. He stopped, opened a light brown box of expensive cigars on the mantelpiece and filled his pockets. Smiling, he took one, bit off the end and lit it. Ben still slumbered. The blonde, still asleep, stirred and moved closer to him. Lacy, placing some of the explosive on the bookshelf, folded a copy of the *Tattler* under his arm. 'There must be some money in here' he thought, but there was no time. He knew that Mustapha would kill him if they awoke. He picked up his bag and departed as quietly as he had entered leaving only the aroma of Cohiba Eslplendido as his mark. He walked down the front stairs and out the front door to the street. It had taken him only seven minutes.

They all sat in the car and after a couple of minutes started up and pulled out. At the end of the street Mustapha gave the signal and the man with the box pushed his thumb down on the white button. They could hear the explosion from the end of the street. Broken glass and rubble filled the air. The man and woman would never know what had hit them. They drove down Brompton Road, through Exhibition Road towards Hyde Park and turned in. They all got out and walked along the pavement until they reached a park bench not far from the bridge near the Serpentine. Lacy lit a cigar and handed two to his accomplices. They all smoked, puffing away and polluting the morning air.

'Too bad there's no scotch' said Lacy in his cockney accent, smiling fiendishly. Mustapha said nothing at first and handed them a wad of American Dollars. A small silence filled the air as they split the money into three and stuffed it in their pockets.

'You know what that means?' Mustapha said.

'Yes...' said Lacy. '...It means America.'

'Yes that's right... America for six months, until the heat is off... I'll send word to you through my people when I get back to Lagos.' He said concluding his instructions. They stood up and the fat man searched his stuffed pockets for a notebook. He took it out and gave it to Mustapha 'Its Bens record of stuff' he said to him, Mustapha took it and wrote something in it. He entered the car and left them. It was time for breakfast.

III

Evening: He was in his suite at the Dorchester. Naked, he stood by the window. There was the smell of *paste laced rolie,* (Tobacco and Cocaine paste Cigarette's) in the air. The Magnum bottle of Krug was almost empty as he stood and watched the lights of cars go past on Park Lane. The two girls had started on themselves again but he had had enough for now. His mind floated him through time backwards to his youth. He could see himself crying by a window in a damp room in Madrid. Crying, his inner tears like rain washed away the pain of his mother's death. That was before all this he thought, before he had come into his own and had become powerful enough to shake the global network of underworld organizations.

TWO

I

With the crack of rifles, three men slumped at the stake. The crowds surged. Men, women, children, beggars, thieves, were held for that still moment when they transcended life. The combat-dressed, red eyed soldiers in a marijuana inspired haze had meted out the punishment

'...Fire!'The shrill sound of the Sergeant-Major's order floated in the air disappearing into the well of spent sound. The white drums echoed the ricochet of off target bullets. They would remain afterwards, a testament to the execution of' Wednesday10th of April, 1985. In his quiet domain a faceless cocaine baron celebrated his triumph. For him, the pressure would be eased, at least for a little while.

One of the dead men whose corpse was carried away to a cheap plywood coffin was only twenty-three. Had he lived, he would still have had hope for a better life, a hope for mercy. His death signaled the start of an investigation into the activities of one man in particular.

II

It would be remembered as one hell of a day for retired Inspector Muna-Muna. 'Kofo come on bring me beer quick!' he said shouting as he emptied the remainder of the froth into the empty beer mug. The still moisture-laden tropical air stifled him as he sweated. He wore only shorts as he sat in his room and parlor dwelling in the slum of Mushin. It was evening and the mosquitoes had awoken for the night drill. He slapped himself all over.

'Come and see blood!' he said gazing at a crushed blood-laden mosquito in his palms. He was on his fourth bottle of Star beer now. 'Be star bright for life!' he mused as he waited for his wife to bring him the fifth bottle.

The dirty gloss pea-green walls of the room seemed to increase the temperature as Muna-Muna looked at himself in the broken mirror that hung askew in front of him. In it he saw his pudgy brown face which reflected his despondent expression. He hadn't bothered to comb his hair or even shave since he had been informed of the sentence passed on his nephew. The small table on which he placed his drink wobbled on the uneven floor as he lifted his glass, a testament to the poor standard of masonry. He sipped the dregs, greedily slurping, from the chipped beer mug. His matronly wife, Kofo, opened the squeaking, rotting timber door, pushed aside the multicolored, stained and worn cotton curtain and brought him the bottle of warm beer.

'Muna; you too like drink o!' She said as she opened the bottle. It hissed and the foam spewed over the neck of the green bottle.

'Na wetin?!' he said, agitated. '…abi man no fit drink again?' and he grabbed the bottle from her and attempted to fill his glass with beer but only succeeded in filling it with foam. He waited a little while and drank the warm beer, relishing the taste of the brew as it trickled down his throat. It had been one hell of a day, he thought, one hell of a day! His nephew, Akin, who had been his ward, had left him today; he had gone, after all the chances that had been given to him; wasted opportunities he thought, a wasted life.

In his cramped bedroom lay the remnants of Akin's possessions: a suitcase full of expensive foreign clothes for which Akin had acquired a taste, and a bag of mementoes, pictures taken at night clubs and parties and letters from various good time girls. Before him as he drank was the twenty-three year olds black address book. Muna meticulously examined every page, address, notation, in the book. He was back to his old style in the police force. He was determined to unravel the mystery, discover the fatal connections that had drawn his nephew into the cocaine business. Until now, like most people in the country, he had never heard of cocaine. The only drugs he had known were 'Chinese capsule' (popularly known as 'mandrax' a tranquilizer) and 'wee wee' (marijuana), and then all of a sudden all this talk of cocaine and heroin had exploded into the limelight. The mosquitoes continued to feed on him and he slapped himself some more. The room darkened as night came. His movements were sloppy, as the beer took its toll; he knocked his glass over and spilt the lager on the worn linoleum floor-covering. He stood, his baggy shorts slipping a little as he paced the cramped sitting room.

'I'm sure he had a girlfriend,' he said to himself. He tried to remember her name. 'Binta that was it, it was Binta!' He flicked the pages of the worn address book quickly and found her name.

'Yes'; he said to himself, I will get to the bottom of this thing.' He took a swig of the warm beer and burped. Then he went to his bedroom and looked for his old pistol.

THREE

MUSTAPHA 1945-1985

By morning, the girls were gone. He went to Stansted airport and boarded his Bombardier Challenger 600. It was South America bound. As they prepared for takeoff, Mustapha rolled some more coca paste and smoked. It was his speed. With his London organization clean he could rest easy, he could be assured that every consignment would be sold at the most profitable prices. He buckled his athletic frame to the seat as the pilot prepared to taxi. He smoked a cigarette mile high as the thrust of the turbojets pushed them across the Atlantic to the new world. The hostess served him dinner and he thought of seducing her. But it only remained a thought. He reverted to his thoughts of the past.

My mother was poor that's why she died; we, like all poor people, were better off dead. I swore that I would never die like her; I would never die unannounced like her I would go with a bang like a king or a president. So I was alone in 1960 for the only beauty in my life was gone. I remember the ship that took me to Panama, it was horrible but the captain and his wife were good. They gave me food even after they found me hiding out on board. It is all clear in my mind, crystal clear.

In Panama I saw hell, not the burning fire but the sort that made one weep tears of poverty and pain. I began by selling cigarettes and fighting in the streets. I killed many men with the knife. I was good with the knife. I can still remember the way it was when I was in the Honduras on the Mosquito Coast. How sweet were the cigarettes and how hot the card tables. But through all that time my soul cried out somewhere for my mother who used to hold me with strong arms, 'everything's going to be right bambino', she would say. She beat me too; she beat me when I said my father was a bastard for leaving us. It is all so clear, so, so, crystal clear. A man outwardly ages but his spirit does not age. I am as I was in Madrid, Panama, Honduras and Columbia. I remember the stacked games and all the card tricks, painstakingly learnt and used to work me towards my success. But it was lonely and I cared for no one. I was alone as we all ultimately are in life. Then I met Romano in a closed game in Costa Rica in '65. The stakes were high and the players were mobsters and eccentric

American millionaires. Romano was with a man called Tuarez, a legendary smuggler of emeralds. Tuarez gambled all over the globe. I played my hands smoothly that night and there were no limits... I won. I had never had it so good. Romano stood by me watching, his face expressionless throughout the game. I cashed my chips and prepared to leave as it was morning. For the first time that evening, Romano spoke. He walked up behind me and said, controlled and unemotionally;

'One second, Mr. Mustapha, just a word. 'We walked into the Gents. I said putting my hands in my pockets and warming my flick knife.

'I will take my money..., Mr. Tuarez money' I held the knife in my palm in my pocket ready to move.

'I can cheat too Mustapha!' He said emphatically, the words had hardly left his lips when I found myself pinned to the ground one knee on my neck and the knife out of my pocket. He was super-fast like a Ninja.

'Okay you win... We can both split it' I said.

'No chance!' he said smiling and took the flick knife off me effortlessly.

That was how I met Romano and I promised to make him pay. In those days I was very hungry, I went after anyone who I had promised to go after with a vengeful passion. Tuarez had a big organization, he was in his fifties; he had the government in his pocket. But he had made a big mistake, the same mistake a champion boxer often makes. He got soft. He had had too many late nights, too much wine, women and pleasures of being famous. A man in his position could not afford to be famous. It weakens, for as a result of this he played to the gallery. He was no longer precise in his activities. He had lost it. He had lost that cold hand, that steely nerve, that 'eye of the tiger.' I noticed this and waited. I waited for the right time. Tuarez was often in Florida in 1969 and I knew that I could get him. If I did I would be king. That is the way it is for a gang is only leadership. No leadership, no gang. I knew that if I killed him I could take over. Tuarez was not too wise. He was clever, but not wise. He had not noticed the discontent among his men. He had been too greedy and there was an air of mutiny in his ranks. He could have averted that if he listened carefully to them, shared some of the good life with his gang. No, he was greedy; he let them watch him and his body guard as they enjoyed the spoils. Greed is a cancer which brings no loyalty as it eats up the body of material wealth.

He had inadvertently napped a little and awoke a little refreshed. He asked for tea and joined the pilot in the cockpit. 'We'll soon start the descent,' he told Mustapha. In the darkness all Mustapha could see were the red lighted wingtips of the aircraft. The plane was now over the Pacific lowlands of Columbia. There, cloaked in the lush rain forest lay a small strip of tar. At the agreed altitude the landing lights were switched on and the pilot caused the aircraft to spiral down and down until the almost invisible array of lights became an airfield in clear vision. Mustapha was soothed by the descent and the sensation caused him to remember his childhood, a children's playground and a long slide. The plane lurched forward a little, bouncing on the tar and then ran sweetly in. Robert Bungham was an excellent pilot.

He taxied the aircraft along with the escort of two jeeps that had been waiting for them, to a camouflaged hangar. They had arrived at Mustapha's hidden home that lay between Bolivar in the hills and the Pacific coast of Columbia. Apart from the airstrip, the only other means of reaching the isolated estate was by boat down the slow meandering River Patia. As the doors of the aircraft were opened, a sticky heat entered the cabin. Mustapha felt it and soon broke out in perspiration. Chico, a driver dressed in a dark green khaki camouflage greeted Mustapha with a warm welcome and they drove off. Mustapha felt like a cold shower. In this processing plant in the middle of the sweating steaming jungle, the Mustapha Organization produced its multi-million dollar commodity. For it was here that coca leaves were refined into concentrated cocaine hydrochloride.

The jeep drove off and took them down a winding gravel road to a large white house. As Bungham looked around the jeep he noticed that the Mustapha Organization had not lowered its paramilitary security measures, Chico was equipped with his usual Israeli machine-gun and he had a few grenades in his belt for good measure. It had always been a difficult business, a ruthless business. They drove down the palm tree lined Avenue to Mustapha's house. It was a large Spanish hacienda-style homestead with beautiful arches, big airy rooms and impeccable marble floors. Even when he was away, as he often was since he had moved to Lagos, the servants, a cook and a steward, kept the house as though he was expected home every evening. Mustapha retired to his rooms after a light dinner, he was tired and was prepared to delay his inspection till the next day.

For two years I waited to hit Tuarez and Romano. I had mobilized my muscle and the plan was set. He was weakest at a card table, we were to organize a high stakes game on board a yacht and my boys would creep up in a paddle boat Jump the security and I'd nab him and snuff him then move in on the emerald trade. It never happened. Things seldom go according to plan. Someone shot him in the head in Florida. Sometimes I'm tempted to think it was Romano, but he was too loyal to Tuarez. It was a mess, a lousy pick-up. In those days emeralds were hotter than cocaine. Anyway, some gringo did him in and wasn't interested in his Columbian set-up, so I moved in, naturally. It took only a few farewells here and there to fix the Tuarez group. Romano had disappeared and no one could trace him, he had many enemies and had gone into hiding. That was so long ago, I was still young then, I had dreams. I thought of the poor and wanted to be like Robin Hood or something. I was out 0f my head. Totally! Power is like cocaine, it blows your mind.

In the morning Mustapha awoke early, still tired and sleepy. He carried with him two watches, one with Lagos time, the other with Columbian time and tried to organize his life between them. He washed, dressed himself in the customary black suit and white shirt without a tie and put on his dark glasses. He wore no jewellery. He took the gold ring that had belonged to his mother and put it in his pocket. He carried it everywhere. Apart from this, he owned nothing that reminded him of the past. His history was in his head and he took great pains to destroy all records and documents. He had strong black coffee and a cigarette. The fat cook came up to him in the dining room.

'Morning, Sir' he said, looking down and avoiding Mustapha's eyes. 'I have prepared you Tortilla Con Jamon.' Mustapha didn't answer; he merely dismissed him with a wave.

In those days I was an amateur. I almost paid for that mistake with my life. I still forgave and trusted. On the hot seat there were several grenades in my organization (Tuarez's Organization) that would shoot me in the back of the head at short notice. One night we went to make a big switch. Five hundred thousand dollars big! We had to sail to the Island of Corona from Mosquera. It was dark. I had my knife with me and also men I thought were my bodyguards. We took an old motor boat from a fisherman in Mosquera and set off for the island. Half a million dollars is enough to kill a President. On our way it started to rain and they made their move. A Little shrimp named Alejandro was their hit man. I had never really noticed them and he told me to stand up and shot me. It was a bad shot, it meant for my head but grazed my neck, there was blood but I fell anyway. He took another shot at me when I was in the water that was a better shot. It hit me in the shoulder. But I was still alive. I was at least ten miles off the coast of Columbia, two wounds, bleeding in shark-infested waters and invisible at night. Even for my swashbuckling proportions it was a long shot and I was in no condition for a long swim. I am sure that an Angel helped me to shore or maybe a dolphin. It is one of the unfilled gaps in my memory as to how I came to be lying on the beach near Tumaco by morning I shall never know. For it had been almost certain that I would die. I was taken in when a fisherman's son found me. They looked after me. Fortunately like Tennessee Williams' Blanche du Bois I too 'have always depended on the kindness of strangers.' When I became strong, penniless, I started again and crawling the coast. In a bar, I met a man I had met before. We were both refugees. Since Tuarez's murder, Romano had been hiding. When he saw me he was warm and told me that I was lucky to be alive. We ate heartily, at his expense. Romano still knew the organization well and we decided to take it back. Like an exiled politician he agreed to reinstate me. We drank cheap wine and he told me of his stay in the United States, he told me of this new drug, cocaine. He said that it was easier than printing money. That was January, 1973 and in two weeks Romano had killed them all; the shrimp Alejandro and his men were dead and I was in control. With Romano of course, I still need him but I think he needs me more. He is a good killer. But that is not all it takes to be a smuggler and the boss.

There was still a morning haze in the air and the veiled sun struggled to warm the land. Mustapha walked out of his villa. He never carried a gun but still had his flick knife strapped to his leg. He walked to the pressing plants that worked day and night. The coca leaves are soaked in a solution which dissolves them and releases the cocaine; they are then pounded into coca paste (as in paste-laced rolie usually smoked with cigarette tobacco). He walked on to a warehouse in which there was a laboratory where the refining of the coca base is performed by a process of combining it with ether and acetone and then filtering it. From here the concentrated cocaine hydrochloride is shipped to his outlets worldwide. He had seen enough, production was working well. He was happy. Once in a while he had to put someone away, say farewell, for it was a difficult business, no one could be trusted for as the money was abundant, betrayal was common. He walked to the chalet where Rob Bungham sat at table for breakfast. He stood.

'Sit down Roberto' Mustapha said gently.

'We've got to leave soon for Lagos.' he continued.

'I am ready to leave, sir' he replied sipping his beer.

'Too early for beer don't you think?' He asked

'Please have some,' Bungham offered and handed him a can of Millers.

'Love the stuff, it's the closest I get to being home... you know the beer reminds me of home.'

'Thanks.' Mustapha said opening the can.

'You're a good guy Roberto... I like you, I will set you up one of these days you'd like a little air charter company of your own back in the States a couple of pipers and a freighter would do the trick, don't worry, Roberto don't worry when I fold up all this, you will get your share, he said tapping gently him on the back. '...Remember, he said in a solemn voice. I am your father and your mother.' Mustapha was mistaken, for he would never get out, he would never sell out. In his business one only got out in a coffin, if you were lucky; usually there was no coffin just a shallow grave. Bungham would never get his air charter company unless he got it now. They drank their beer and arranged to leave at noon.

By 12.30 they were airborne. He felt a certain joy at going back to Lagos. He had never really had a home and he had adopted the capital of the country often called the 'Giant of Africa' as his home. It was different from any other place he had been to. It was alive, wild and alive that is Africa, the living continent. Lagos fitted his idea of life, it was a place that could kill a man or sharpen his senses. True, only the fittest survived. But anyway, he would have been under pressure anywhere else in the world. He relaxed in the spacious seat and stared at the video screen, having already missed half of the film. A red light flashed on the console beside him and he picked up the telephone receiver.

'It's Musa from Zurich sir' Bungham said through the small speaker.

'Switch him on,' Mustapha replied. They talked quickly, in almost meaningless terms.

'I hope it's all in Musa, I will see you in Lagos.' He said before he dropped the phone, it's easy to run a country he thought, money opens all doors. He took a paste-laced roiled from the cigarette case and smoked, it calmed him.

He asked for some tea and he smoked again. There were bags beneath his vacant eyes. The stress was taking its toll on him. The past is gone he thought, gone into the bowels of time and was history and he decided to leave all unanswered questions of the past unanswered. As he sat, he began to think of Binta. Sometimes she crept into his thoughts and he couldn't help but think of her. He smiled to himself as he remembered the days when he was obsessed with her. He still liked her though, but it was not so passionately. It was Friday 19th April, 1985 as they headed for Lagos.

FOUR

1ST SEPTEMBER 1980

A gentle breeze caressed Musa Ahmed as he sat relaxed on the balcony of his hotel suite in Victoria Island. He smoked as he looked across the almost unruffled shimmering water at the wharf on Tin Can Island. His eyes, quick and alive, darted about indicating an inner unease. It was easy to tell that his suave exterior and dark, beautiful, almost feminine face was merely a disguise. It was required that he, as an officer of the army intelligence corps, appeared as almost harmless.

Major Musa Ahmed would most probably have succeeded in any other type of endeavor to which he may have directed himself. Because he had, as part of the winning formula, the magic factor about him, that extra quality that makes a man succeed in spite of his circumstances. Unlike other members of the intelligence corps who were usually avoided, he was popular with both officers and men. This was apparent from the fact that he never lacked drinking partners. They, the other officers and the men who often kept his company, did not necessarily think that was a great talker or that he could be confided in, but like all military men in the present armed forces, they always wanted to be on the winning team.

He looked at his watch and noted that it was just coming to seven o'clock in the evening; the sea breeze filled the room behind, lifted the large white curtain and blew it about like a ship's sail. He stood up, tall, lithe and noble looking in his cream French suit, walked gently and deliberately over the marble floor and pile carpets from the balcony through the suite to the fridge in the kitchenette. He returned with a silver bucket, a chilled bottle of champagne and a fluted crystal glass with a black stem. Unlike traditional Muslims he had no reservations about alcohol or about several other things. He opened the bottle expertly with a suppressed pop and filled his glass. As he sipped the cold wine, the nectar of his desires, he could hear the shrill melodies from the quivering trumpeter whose soulful blast led the highlife band that played at the bar beside the pool in the garden of the hotel. There was a sharp knock on the door and Musa a little startled, walked into the green suite, took his pistol, a browning automatic, from the drawer in the bedside table, removed the safety catch and walked silently towards the door carefully avoiding any direct line of fire.

'Whom do you want?' he said calmly as he crept beside the wall.

'I want Major Musa, I came to seek him', a young voice said cryptically.

Musa, aware that this was no assailant, relaxed a little and put the pistol along with his right hand in his trouser pocket and opened the door.

'I am Akin sir… I was sent by a man in Surulere.' The young fresh faced man at the door said

'Come …'Musa said in his northern accented clear English.

The young man walked into the room, his faded blue jeans frayed in parts, looking out of place. He looked eighteen or nineteen and had a handsome flawless face. He appeared a little apprehensive; his full lips pouted indignantly, betrayed his disposition. On the surface he appeared much like any other fresh-faced youth, but his eyes, brown distant orbs were archives of experience that indicated that he was not so fresh faced. Musa, aware that the boy was not relaxed, tried to make him comfortable.

'Chamfagne?' he offered.

'Thank you' Akin answered.

Musa filled him a glass which he drank quickly, a little greedily and he lit a cigarette from the gold packet of Benson and Hedges. As he exhaled he felt better. He had been a little afraid of meeting this man called Musa, but his hunger reminded him that he should persevere. He stared in awe at the plush suite and wondered when and if he would ever be able to afford such luxury. It occurred to him that it was all perfect, it all blended, the suite, the wine, the gentle sea air and the distant highlife music.

Musa stared at him, Musa's eyes also exposed his past, and his burning pupils showed that he had swum through a sea of sharks to reach his present position. The Major's eyes though, had something else in them, they betrayed ambition. He was not done yet; he still had a long way to go. Slowly, after several glasses they were both relaxed, Musa replaced the bottle with another and they continued drinking.

'You know what our business is?' Musa asked.

'Yes' Akin replied confidently.

'In that case I don't have to exflain to you how dangerous it can be' Musa said mixing his p's and f 's.

'Yes I know about danger'

Musa smiled a little sardonically, he, being the more experienced, was all too aware of danger.

But Akin was no amateur and had been well schooled in Lagos. He had kept the company of criminals and had taken part in petty theft, pick-pocketing and other illicit activities. He had been in a remand home a couple of times when he was still a minor; it had only made him worse. He was the product of a fast growing city, which through urban migration and oil money was an expanding squalor, the consequence of which was crime. His generation, the youth, was steeped in the pursuit of money and he like the majority of petty thieves was street wise. He didn't realize though that he had just ventured out of his depth.

'Tomorrow morning... Musa said '...You will meet a man here in Victoria Island, I will tell you where, he will be your boss, his name is Romano' he will give you everything you need, a fassfort... anything.'

'Yes Sir... Thank you!'

Akin smoked another cigarette. He thought of his past, his short life; his mother had brought him up alone as she had been a concubine to the village head. It was a small village in which everyone knew everything about everyone else. He had been cared for by his mother and aunts. He often thought of her, his mother, big and warm and he could smell her as she had cuddled him when he cried. He remembered the gentle way in which she had taken care of him and told him 'don't mind them they jealous you!' when the other children had laughed at him. He had been in the local school until his mother had left him almost alone in the world when she died after a severe tropical illness which led to the collapse of both her kidneys. That was when he came to Lagos, at the age of eleven, to live with his aunt a childless nurse. She was a strict woman and even though he had tried hard to live up to her expectations, she wanted too much from him and he had failed to be a good son or ward, He was hopeless at school where he learnt nothing due to his constant absences and he soon fell into bad company. He began with kai-kai and beer and then spent his day's playing cards with the *Malams* and smoking marijuana in the evenings. He had started early, at fifteen, to descend into the wells of iniquity. His visions changed as did most of his ideas, and his village, his mother that loved him, all seemed to be part of a fairy tale, a distant and hazy memory. Those memories still touched him though; they injected his frustrations with an innocence that he had long lost.

Musa Ahmed felt himself becoming more aware of Akin as he stared at him through the haze of cigarette smoke he exhaled. It had been a while; he had been working hard recently and had little time for relaxation. He licked his lips as he imagined himself in the throes of sodomy.

'You like the Chamfagne?' Musa asked him'… good Chamfagne is the best, if you like it I can give you a carton here take this buy yourself anything you want, wine, food anything' Musa said thrusting a thick wad of Naira notes to Akin.

'Thank you' Akin said, quickly stuffing it in the back pocket of his jeans.

'You like cigars?' Musa asked.

'I never smoked cigars…'

'Here take a few from this box, King Edwards' cigars, verri good, take, take…'

Akin took a handful and placed them on the table beside him.

He stiffened a little, becoming Suspicious of the generosity of the stranger. Musa stood up walked around and then sat down next to Akin on the sofa. He put his hand over his shoulders squeezing him.

'We will be good friends, you and me good friends? Yes? Yes? Good friends Ok?'

'Yes we will be friends,' Akin said.

'Good, good....' Musa said slapping him intimately on the back.'... good, good,' he repeated.

He filled Akin's glass with more bubbly and they both smiled at each other; Musa's face lit up deviously. He pulled Akin's head close to his and whispered softly into his ear.

'Take something more, let's get high and go out somewhere, Peninsula, Lords? Anywhere you want to go, we will find nice women?'

'Yes Women.' Akin nodded, he relaxed a little. Musa was alright, nothing to be afraid of, no, nothing at all be afraid of, he was just a fun loving guy he thought, he was now convinced that all the stories he had so often and about military officers and their being fun loving were true.

'What kind of women do you like?' Musa asked.

'I like big women,' Akin said women

'I like big, buxom women'

'Yes, yes...big breasted women!'

'That's punny punny?'

'Funny? That is wild man!' Akin said smiling broadly.

'Have more have more Chamfagne!' Musa said with a command as he filled his glass to the brim Chamfagne is the best it's the best!' Musa said almost screaming, he was getting drunk.

'So where's the stuff man?' Akin asked trying to sound trendy.

'What... stuff?'

'Hey you said high, let's get high?'

You want smoke... or dust?'

'Hell let's smokes'

Musa walked off unsteadily. He returned with the marijuana. Akin lit it, the pungent smoke obscuring his face as he puffed, he handed it to Musa who smoked too, coughing a little. They both smoked, exchanging the weed cigar until it was finished. Akin lit a cigarette.

'Hey, Musa...I'm cool, I'm cool.' He said unconvincingly. 'Do you want to see some magazines?'

What magazines?' Akin asked rolling his head from side to side.

'Come, come… come see…' Musa said as he walked into the bedroom.

He opened a drawer, found several magazines, the kind with naked people in them and flung them on the bed.

'You can see in these women with big breasts,' he said. Akin thumbed through '*Playboy*', and '*Oui*' and '*Men only*'

'Yeah, that's wows look at these... come and see this chick!' he said between the glossy pictures.

Musa sat down on the bed, pulled the drawer of the bedside table and took out a small silver pill box and a small spoon.

'Have you tried this?' Musa asked as he took small Sharp sniffs of the powder.

'What? Hey… hell why not, let me go too' Akin said as Musa helped him snort some

'This is crazy, really crazy!' He said as he sneezed.

Musa relaxed, lay face up on the bed and stared at the ceiling.

'Let's go and get some girls', Akin said.

'We don't need girls.' Musa said almost whispering

'Who said that?' Akin said.

'Come on… you are a fine boy!' Musa said reaching over to him and holding his head.

Musa stood up and undressed, removing his top. He was slim with stringy athletic muscles. Akin was disoriented by the evening's intake; he shivered a little as he lay confused, unable to remember where he was, and with whom.

'Come on, take off your clothes!' Musa commanded

'What?'

'Take them off!' Musa said truculently in a desperate animal voice, he held in his hand a leather horse whip which he had taken from a drawer beside his bed. Musa's eyes gleamed as he swung the whip making it whistle in the air. Akin's resistance was minimal, he felt the pain as the whip came down on him and he felt his clothes being removed from his body, is Musa kicked him and pushed him. Tears came up in his eyes, streamed down his face and he died a thousand times.

In the morning he staggered to the bathroom to examine himself. As he looked at his bruised body, cut lip and torn clothes, he realized that it was not quite as easy as he imagined. Later he limped away debased and dehumanized with a pocket full of colored paper. He had met the first of the little devils.

FIVE

LAGOS *19th APRIL* 1985

Romano Moreno walked around the departure lounge. He always awaited Mustapha's arrival. Mustapha was most vulnerable when he travelled and was not surrounded by his usual protection of bodyguards and security men. Romano meandered through the islands of baggage: boxes, cartons, suitcases, clothes, bundles of stuffed sacks and other unimaginable packages more suited to a camel's back than the hold of an aircraft. He was lost in the sea of brown faces in the hall. Like his employer, he was an outsider and it was at times like this that this fact was most apparent. The air conditioners were not cooling well and the heat, spurred by the multiplied body heat caused the hall to be humid. He removed his jacket, exposing a sweat soaked Sea Island cotton shirt that stuck in patches to his stocky frame. He was well built and short, a deceptive body guard; at five foot five he was a little small but he was really very fast and apart from being adept at the use of firearms, he could kill with his bare hands, a knife or any other object.

His brown eyes were shielded by the veneer of dark sunglasses; his scarred face, tanned and roughhewn by nature and combat, was evidence of his occupation. He stopped, wiped the perspiration from his brow with a handkerchief and ran his fingers backwards through his short cropped brown hair, which was balding at the temples. Like Mustapha his expression and his disposition were ceramic. He looked at his watch and walked towards the arrival gate to which they had been assigned. The Customs and Immigration officials knew him well and allowed him a free run of the building. Money was power. It was 11.00 p.m. and the message from the aircraft had informed them of Mustapha's arrival. Romano Moreno was born in Mexico City thirty-eight years earlier but he looked older than his years. The late nights, alcohol and action had taken their toll. He was also orphaned at an early age. His parents had been of peasant farming stock, he was one of the lucky few who had broken away, by whatever means, from the trap into which they were born. Before he had joined Tuarez he was arrested in Mexico at the age of nineteen for counterfeiting. He had escaped from detention with the aid of the members of Tuarez's gang and slipped through the mountain passes to Guatemala where he gambled poorly and changed his trade to muscle. His feats in bars not only earned him a reputation as a great fighter but also left him with the scar of several stitches on his right cheek. The man that hurt him did not live long after that. He was eventually sought by the best. Tuarez crowned him with the title of 'the bodyguards' bodyguard.'

But that was all such a long time ago. In the heat of the modern African airport he was an outsider in control. So it is in the country, perpetually, even though ostensibly independent, a plunderer's land. He had come here six years ago, after helping Mustapha to establish the Columbian processing Plant. The flexibility of bureaucracy and the law along with the mad obsessive pursuit of wealth by the people, a consequence of the new oil wealth, had made it an ideal place for the trafficking of hard drugs. Romano and Mustapha had invested in an assembly plant for motorcycles and had in so doing acquired residency permits. The drug trade had been very small before their arrival. It had been mainly confined to the trafficking of marijuana, which in the international network was reserved for amateurs. In five years they had infiltrated the government and the military, created a few millionaires and even threatened the stability of certain entrenched individuals. But how long would it last, he wondered. They had to focus their eyes on new land to which they could transfer and further build their empire.

Romano, in the recesses of his dreams sought an organization of his own From which he could retire to bliss as he weakened, like all men, ebbing towards his death. He was a thinker for short moments only, and he snapped out of it to face reality. He had heard through the network of informants that Ben had been killed, blown to pieces in his sleep. Mustapha always found a new, effective, almost traceless way every time. He feared Mustapha as a boxer fears his adversary, both having knowledge of what damage could be done to each other. He lit a cigarette out of habit, smoking it automatically not savoring it in any way. He looked at his watch impatiently waiting for the plane to land. Mustapha was usually a little late or a little early. It made it difficult for his movements to be easily monitored.

SIX

19th April, 1985

She woke early and went downstairs for a coffee. All were asleep in the household except for her father who, as a devout Muslim, always awoke early for his prayers. She sat beside the telephone sipping coffee and waiting for the call, she wondered about this man, Inspector Muna-Muna, who had left several messages and had promised to telephone at the odd hour of six a.m. She would not have bothered if he had not said that that he was Akin's uncle. Akin's death still seemed unreal to her. Although she had seen the news reports in the papers, it still had not sunk in. She was waiting, in a half-hearted hope, for a miracle, half expecting him to walk into the room, alive. But it was a forlorn hope, she knew, somewhere inside of her heart that he was gone and that nothing could ever bring him back. And she had prayed, albeit half-hartedly, for God to change the circumstances. She had, on account of Akin's death, blamed God.

To her, He was the one that was responsible for everything. And it occurred to her that she and all of humanity were small. Like ants in a world of men, almost meaningless. She also felt helpless, having no control over her future. She wondered how much Mustapha had to do with it all, why hadn't Mustapha protected him. She continued to ask herself. He could have, quite easily, helped him out even after his arrest. It was all so sinister. It was almost quiet there in the house, the sound of singing birds that came in from the grey garden as day broke, the sound of cars filtered by the trees, their motors running by, from the street. But still there was in the room a strange silence, she was alone there with her God, the ever present and all powerful, the puppeteer, controlling the aging world in the seemingly perpetual battle between good and evil, as the crossfire blew the human pawns across the checkered war board, damning their wretched lives. It was almost 6.00 a.m.

Binta Yar Mouktar was petite with large brown twinkling eyes that could soften a heart of stone. She was the daughter of Usman Yar Mouktar, a wealthy Alhaji from Zuru in Sokoto State. He was now Chairman of a bank and they all lived in Lagos. She was, by her father's position, a child of the Northern Elite and consequently had been educated at Roedean, a prestigious school for girls in England. Her English, etiquette and aquiline facial features were impeccable. As were her fresh face, flawless complexion and clear eyes. She had the aura and grace of a model when she walked. When she met Mustapha in September of 1980, she neither smoked nor drank alcohol. She had since fallen from grace. Day broke gently in the tropical garden and grey gave way to blue and blue to white until the glaring yellow of sunlight lighted all. It was already eight o'clock and he had not called. She no longer thought about the telephone, she didn't care, but sitting there in the morning watching the world awaken had stirred up the past in heart and allowed her subconscious to creep into her conscious. She remembered the past in patches. And it touched her. In her mind she could see the past, the party, it had all happened so quickly at the party. She had been introduced by a friend to Mustapha. She remembered him asking her, 'Have you been to France?

'No' she had said.

'Let's go there,' he had said quite casually.

She had thought that he was pulling her leg and as such had played along to amuse him. 'Yes; she had answered when he asked her if she liked the south of France. She had said that she'd heard so much about it and had always wanted to go. 'It's all fixed for tomorrow then?' he had asked. She had agreed and he had promised to send a car round the next morning. She, like many in the city, had never heard of Mustapha. The next morning a silver Mercedes had pulled up to the front of her house in Ikoyi. She had, in good humour, agreed to see the joke to its end. She had been taken in the car to the airport and all the while she had found his humor, Mustapha's, very exciting. She had been taken right unto the Apron to a little white jet 'Inside,' the driver had said 'Mustapha's is inside' and from the cockpit Bungham In dark sunglasses gave her a thumbs up sign as she walked past and was ushered up the stairs. Mustapha was already in the plane and the jets whined into life, Mustapha gave Bungham the go ahead as he welcomed her to sit beside him. He was dressed in his white kaftan and was eating pistachios and drinking wine. She remembered it so clearly

'I thought you might have refused to come,' he had said as she sat down. Minutes later, they were airborne.

That was how she had started with 'Mustie'. Her education had essentially been an initiation into the material world. It may be granted though that this process was sprinkled with a veneer of intellectuality and as such she could sometimes, when she sought to

prove that she was educated, discuss such topics as the writings of Emily Bronte and the persecution of Huguenots in France and of course Western and African art. But she was ignorant of life itself and by her condition, she was ripe to fall prey to a man like Mustapha who could almost buy whatever he wanted in the world. He was able to satisfy all her material and physical fantasies and as such, she had thought that she loved him. And compounded with her material greed was an ignorance of men and as she had never been allowed and had never succeeded in effectively having an affair before Mustapha, she knew nothing of men's tricks and the lies they could tell.

She went upstairs, having decided to face the day, and showered quickly, she dressed in white slacks, a blue T-shirt and an over blown cotton print jacket by Betty Jackson. She wore gold and ivory chunky bangles, a dab of perfume and put on her dark sunglasses and canvas espadrilles. She was still sad and decided to take a drive in her Volkswagen cabriolet, a present from Mustapha. It was eleven and the yellow tropical heat burned down on her, had she been happier she would have gone for a swim. She started up and headed towards Ikorodu Road via the Third Mainland Bridge. There was no silence about her and the city, like a beehive, was overrun with activity; the yellow *molues* with sardine-packed passengers carried the poor about, the rich, and the not so rich were either chauffeur driven or in taxis, school children wandered about in truancy and somewhere in the city, surely, a married woman and her lover met in a hidden room in a quiet hotel in the immoral city. Driving was her only therapy and she drove quickly. She played loud music boosted through fidelity amplifier and the bass beat rocked her heart. She took from her cigarette case, a cigarette laced with coca paste and smoked, the soft top was down and the wind rushed through her hair, her jacket, and her breasts. Her eyes were shielded from the dust and sunshine and as she raced, switching from lane to lane, she could feel life. She had held it long enough and could hold it no longer, her throat tightened, tears trickled down behind her ray bans and she tasted the salt on her lips 'Akin, Akin, Akin…' she said sobbing 'what a rotten world this is, what a rotten, rotten world!'

She put her foot down, moving faster! She was lonely and she let her tears soothe her, ease her emotions. She momentarily felt the cowardly impulse of suicide, she suppressed it, and it passed. It was a wonder how life could dictate actions. She was not by nature a coward, but, like all, she had in the recesses of her heart that fear of challenging and traumatic situations in life. But somehow it still came through, that will to live, to survive even through the worst of tragedies. Her mind went back to the past.

They had landed at Orly airport, hurried through all the formalities and had been treated with that respect which was usually reserved for only the very famous, and of course, the very rich. They had been quickly whisked away from the customs office to a black Mercedes waiting outside, in which all the rear windows had been blacked out and a chauffeur up front with a stone faced man with burly shoulders. Mustapha always required a bodyguard. He was a target, at all times, for his competitors. As the returns in the business were staggering, a man's life hardly meant much. They had stayed at the Le Meurice hotel where Mustapha kept a suite. The hotel suited him as it made provisions which allowed him a pantry and kitchen for his personal chef.

'Your clothes...' he had said'... you came unprepared, you have no clothes'. He had been only too willing to spend some of his abundant money on her and took her out shopping. He took her to the Rue du Faubourg St Honore and bought, after she had made her choice, beautiful and expensive clothes; dresses by Chloe, a little red suit from Chanel and dresses from Kritzia and other famous names. He even bought her a swimsuit by Norma Kamali for dipping in the Mediterranean. He always paid cash, not being a man for records, credit cards and checks, which were eventually, stored in the indelible memory banks of the world's computers. But, all in all, the prize of his first material bequests was from Cartier; a gold necklace with lapis lazuli beads and a diamond clasp. She had been, after shopping, equipped to go to dinner. He took her to an exclusive and quiet restaurant on the Rue Lamennais where they dined in quiet elegance and luxury; she displayed on her slim neck her Cartier. Back at the hotel, when they returned, he made love to her; from then on, he made her understand that he believed it was physically the woman's condition, to give pleasure to her man. After a couple of days they had gone on to the south of France and the remaining two days there at the Hotel Cap at. In the quiet tranquility of the nineteenth century villa Mustapha made love to her again and again, tirelessly.

And she began to understand the relativity of the flesh. She thought, in the blitz of romance and material fulfillment that she began to love him. But, in retrospect, she was out of her depth and the hazy distant expression in his eyes she mistaken for love and fondness. She should have taken heed when one evening as they dined at the Eden Roc he had said most casually and harmlessly 'I possess, when I want to make use of it, a great capacity for evil...' She had laughed at the time but, when all is said and done, Mustapha was in love with her. He was in love only in such a way as much as he could be in love at all; it was more a personal style of love mainly made up of a limited and self-controlled caged emotion. His ceaseless pursuit of money and power had eroded his sensibilities and he could feel very little. That was the price, for there is a price in everything men do; like the hand of God it hangs over man like the sword of Damocles ready to slice away its pound of flesh. Mustapha, the money and power inspired automaton was unable to feel love, the most precious of all jewels. After four days in France, they had returned to Lagos and on the night flight home he held her in his arms and told her about himself, almost, for he hardly confided and only used confidence as tool for leverage. He had planned it; he did all the right things to make her his emotional slave. He was, even in romance, a shrewd and cunning businessman.

'My mother... he had said 'died a pauper my father, on the other hand, to me has never died, he has also never lived.' I am what people would call a bastard.' He had a subtle and devious way of masking the truth. But she was ignorant, and had been quite happy to only listen. By her foreign education she had been instilled with the belief that a woman must fall in love and she contrived it.

He had not told her what his business was; it was inevitable that she found out, as there is nothing that remains hidden under the pillow of lovers. But he was expert in his manipulation of the truth for he told very few lies. He made sure that whatever he told her had some thread of truth in it. He stretched the little truth that there was and painted a colorful picture of his past life and his assent to the 'power and the glory' consequently she created a hero of him.

She decided to turn off left into the airport road and head for the Country Club. It was a place that held memories for her as she had often met Akin there; it. Was neutral ground and in those days was unlikely that she would he seen with him there. She went to the bar and ordered a tomato juice. It was almost empty, since it was a working day, but there was in the corner, a group of sweating Europeans visibly hooked on Star beer. She drank her tomato juice slowly, savoring its bitter sweet qualities. She wondered how she had come to have her life; its events and turns, mixed up with those of a man like Mustapha whose adventures were reserved for the pages of a cheap novel. A fat customs officer walked in took off his cap settled down alone for a drink. Binta asked for another juice with gin in it and watched him, the customs Officer, as he drank his beer at lightning speed. He was a jolly looking fat man one of those roly poly sorts, the kind that his friends would call out to jovially 'fattie how your belle de?!' He glanced at her in passing, like most men did, acknowledging her beauty. He was young with a happy thick-mustached face from which he wiped froth with the back of his hand. The fingers on his hands were adorned with jewelry she noticed large gold rings when he waved his hands commanding the barman.

'Bar man! Bring another beer quick-quick... you think say time go wait? ... I have to be at Murtala Mohammed when the London flight comes in!' he said with an air of authority, she looked away and fiddled with her drink.

The air was quite still and in it hung the exhaust fumes of passing cars, the smells of the city. She thought about how she had come to know Mustapha, how he slowly revealed his life to her. He had shown her more and power than she had ever imagined in her dreams. She could not even begin to calculate how much money he was worth, from what she saw of his business methods, neither could he. But, from observing him, she was aware that his lust, for that is what it was, animal lust, was insatiable. She knew that he wanted everything, she knew that since he could not have everything he would die trying and so would any that stood in his way.

To paint all her memories of her beginnings with Mustapha as memories of deception would be wrong. She remembered it like a montage, in bits, and sometimes the good bits came too. She could also remember golden days, full of blue sky, white clouds, lots of fresh air and happiness. She could remember days on the beachfront in Takwa Bay open to the Atlantic where the surf bubbles on white sand wetting it, and turning it brown. She could remember swimming with Mustie, living, enjoying herself. It wasn't so bad at times when she remembered. She looked at her finger at her diamond ring and it was not so beautiful, the solitaire, reminding her of her loneliness, her lost love.

Deep inside her she felt a little hunger and fear. It was not wise for her to remain alone as she could bring harm upon herself. She watched the fat man leave and she asked for another drink which she rushed before she left, going home to a message that awaited her. She needed friends, shoulders to lean on, to cry on. She had been envied by many in competitive and materialistic Lagos society because of her relationship with Mustapha and she had no real friends. That was the most difficult thing for her at this time, for she was sure that it would have been easier if she could share her grief with someone else, a shoulder to cry on, a friend is most valued when you are in trouble and in need of one. It can be a cruel and lonely world. At home, when she got there; a written message from Inspector Muna-Muna awaited her.

'It is about Akin....' it read 'I shall come to talk to you about him, please await me at 10.00 a.m. tomorrow.'

She tore it into little pieces, as it confirmed to her the truth; that Akin's death was not a dream. She sought sleep; at least it could hold and suspend her grief. She took a glass of water, 5 milligrams of valium and went to sleep.

SEVEN

ZURICH *19TH APRIL* 1985 5.00 pm

In his plush hotel suite in Zurich, Major Musa Ahmed dropped the telephone after having just spoken to Mustapha 'five million dollars!' He thought speaking out the words to himself, relaxing on the chaise longue and stretching himself like a cat. He was pleased at the progress that had been made in the arrangement. He would have enough money to pay large bribes freeze army signals, hold the Air force and even arrange that the radio should be off the air for a while. He felt elated at the prospect of power. All his life he had been determined to harness political power and ride it like Bonaparte on a magnificent white horse, he could hardly wait to have the reins in his hands.   A plan formed in his mind as he dreamt; at the appointed time on the specified day, the activities would begin. In the early hours of the morning he would dispatch several trucks full of armed soldiers to the residences of the service chiefs and other important senior military personnel.

Their task would be to kidnap them under the pretext that they had been summoned by the Head of State. If, unfortunately for them, they refused to cooperate and would not be taken alive, then their instructions would be to kill them on the spot. Simultaneously, he would have sent other troops to the main radio stations and the telephone exchanges. Meanwhile Musa and his closest aides would take hold of the airport and via shortwave from the control room, he would make his takeover speech at dawn.

This arrangement was also a cunning insurance for Musa Ahmed, a trained pilot, as it allowed him to hijack and escape with an aircraft to Switzerland and the funds which he had deposited there in the event of failure. He walked over to a writing table and sat. He had long been obsessed with the planning of a coup d'état, it had over the years become the life force that drove him, pumping through his veins like high octane fuel into a turbocharger. And he had books on the past Independence coups; he had books on the two coups of 1966, the coup of 1975, the attempt of 1976. He read also about the life of Cromwell, the military genius of Gustavus Adolphus and Genghis Khan. Bonaparte was his hero and he admired also Che's book on Guerilla warfare which he had read several times. From his array of literature he extracted what he thought were the essential principles that would guarantee his success. As he stood and walked round the beautiful room which was furnished with Louis XVI pieces, his mind went to the future. It would all end soon, he thought, it would soon be over, this life of insignificance, this cloak and dagger stuff. He would become a man of great importance. In his country he would arrive at functions in a long motorcade with outriders heralded by sirens, guarded with tanks and followed by plush cars. The people would stop their work, their cars, bicycles; school children would line up and wave to him as he passed by. In foreign countries he would be treated like king. He would meet the most influential people in the world on equal terms. He would have people groveling at his feet begging to pimp for him. He stared in the mirror at his image. Nice he thought, very nice. He would soon have world famous photographers clamoring for a chance to take pictures of him. He would have only the best take his portrait; maybe even a famous artist would paint him. It was always important to project the right image. He would have the best public relations specialists recommend how best his image would be projected. He would be cut above all previous leaders, civilian or military, 'It was time we had a man with style,' he said to himself 'time we had a man with style' he repeated, talking to himself.

But he deceived himself; he was misled in his dreams since he knew nothing of power. For apart from the execution of the takeover plot, he would be totally unprepared to rule as he knew nothing about the machinery of government. He would be unable to handle power and consequently would become a stony faced figure displayed in the back of a fleeting black Mercedes. He would constantly be dancing to the tune of foreign capitalists knowing little or nothing about governing a people other than stealing money and sharing it with his accomplices in the administration for doing nothing; a ten percent government. And he was shortsighted for he could not hope to stay in power for long, he would be watched by one like him in the forces who aspired to his position and the cycle would repeat itself again and again in the process of unending military coups.

He took a cigarette from his platinum cigarette case, lit it and exhaled watching the blue grey smoke float in shapeless wisps as it caught the yellow light from the lamp, his mind still concentrated on a plan. He would make sure he took care of Mustapha once he became Head of State. It was foolish to have ones benefactor looking over one's shoulder. He would use all the security services to wipe Mustapha away. It could be done easily he thought, be able to use the law, trap him with some retroactive Decree and then finish him off.

He could even use Romano, why not, every man has his price, and Romano must have his. The idea of using Romano appealed to him. Yes, he thought Just like Judas, the closest were always the most dangerous. And he set his mind on how it should be done; he smiled to himself as he plotted the fall of Mustapha. It was what he did best, the planning of betrayal.

EIGHT

FRIDAY *19 APRIL* 1985

It was dark. Mustapha awoke as the plane circled above starship-lit runway awaiting permission to land. Romano, awaiting his arrival, had grown impatient and had smoked several tasteless cigarettes. He scratched his scalp as the night heat affected him.

'They are here, sir,' a customs officer said

'…Just about to land…' He continued, nodding and humming as he walked aimlessly about the baggage. Bungham brought the Challenger down perfectly. He was really a wonderful pilot. He taxied to the appropriate position and stopped. Mustapha hurried down the stairs and up the spiral staircase into the finger. He walked briskly as the humid heat bounced up at him. Without fuss they raced through all the formalities and walked through to the idling Mercedes.

'Have you heard?' Mustapha asked stiffly as he shut the door.

'We have heard.' Romano replied solemnly.

It was a dark night, there was no moon, no stars, and as usual little light, they moved quickly as it was unsafe go slowly through the city traffic at this time, sometimes Lagos could be unsafe. Mustapha lit a cigarette; there were bags under his eyes, he felt tired. Every bone in his body seemed to weigh like lead and his muscles, like a puppet's strings, hung to his aching frame. The two watch trick hadn't worked so well. Romano replaced his pistol in its holster from the pocket in which he had kept it in the car.

The authorities would allow them anything but guns in the airport. Mustapha rolled his neck in an attempt to soothe it. His mind travelled and as the tires rolled, making a hollow humming sound on the smooth asphalt. He thought again of the past, his mind flashed from his childhood to his mother, to Binta, from Binta to the party, money, to Musa, Romano, life, death, Binta's life, time! He felt as if he was losing his grip, after this he would take a warm bath, a brandy and lots of deep sleep.

'Have you got a rolie…' he asked his voice a little hoarse.

'Yes.' Romano said flatly then he fumbled with the cigarette box and finding him the usual smoke. Mustapha took it.

'Give me a light!' He said.

'…give me a light!' he repeated.

Romano flicked his lighter and lit both the rolie and illuminated the interior of the car for a brief moment. He noticed Mustapha's shaking hands. Even in the cool air-conditioned interior of the car Mustapha felt hot, he was perspiring. He inhaled forcefully, the acrid smoke drying his throat. The feeling of the drug came slowly, he calmed, and he inhaled again.

'We have got to see Musa Ahmed… he's due back tomorrow…tell him to come … find him the minute he lands and tell him to come… tell Noga too!' Mustapha instructed. He was tired now and his voice weakened. His mind, no longer in control was blank, as his eyelids, heavy with sleep, closed slowly.

There was a sharp metallic clang! The car veered! Mustapha awoke.

'What in hell!' He screamed.

The front tires were deflated by the object and the driver struggled to control the Mercedes as it careered into concrete buffer on the Bridge. There were no cars in sight, they were alone. Romano, alert at the events was ready to spring into action and he pulled out his pistol. The car stopped and the driver slumped injured on the steering wheel.

'Shit!' Romano yelled as he opened his door and rolled out of the car into a face down shooting position. A tall dark bare-chested man in shorts stood at a distance of about fifty or sixty meters and fired two shots into the still night air.

Mustapha, still in the car, slid down in his seat and groped under the front seat in search of his loaded pistol. He found it, removed the safety catch, let himself stealthily out of the car and assumed the same position as Romano. Behind them, traffic in the distance had stopped and reversed in frenzy. Most drivers in Lagos watched out keenly for armed robbery incidents, carjacking and assassination situations and were ready to react immediately. Mustapha could see four men emerging from the darkness running towards them.

'Wait I say...' Mustapha said 'wait until I say shoot!' He commanded. The men still running approached their quarry. They stopped. Seeing the figures on the road and fired several careless and off-target shots. Sharp cracks of rapid gunfire rang into the night.

'Now...!' Mustapha screamed 'Now!'

They both took three shots each; accurately. The four approaching men fell; one of them lay on the road shaking, twitching before he breathed his last and died. Romano sprang like a cat; he got up, ran towards them in a zigzag and shot the three surviving assailants in the head at point blank range.

The hunted hunters had survived again. They both carried the hurt driver, one on either side of him; they walked on the Eko Bridge towards Lagos Island. Mustapha, still tired, thought of his hot bath and brandy. Sometimes he hated life in this country, he thought, the heat, the life; a feral land. He looked over the bridge toward the lagoon at the array of lights that twinkled like fallen stars in the squalor of the over-populated city.

'I hope he's alright' Mustapha said 'He was a good driver!' Mustapha said almost screaming. Romano didn't speak for a while and he panted under the weight of the unconscious man. A little later, he spoke. 'We must tell Musa about this when he returns... I'm sure he'll clear it all up.'

He wondered if the assailants had really been armed robbers attacking them at random. It didn't matter too much, really; whoever they had been, they were dead.

NINE

SEPTEMBER 1980

After France he had taken her over. Binta could make no move without Mustapha and sometimes she even felt he had her watched. To him she had become a weakness and he found that he could deny her nothing; exquisite clothes, jewels, a car and elaborate posh parties. He had little else to do with his ever growing illicit wealth. He took her in hand, as a master to the apprentice, and opened her eyes to the world, to his twinkling world of money and power. She had been little known among the small but exclusive elite that dominated the city, but, as a result of Mustapha's bequests, she became a target for envy. Her flamboyant entertaining was often the topic of discussion at the gossip sessions of the little rich girls of Ikoyi and Victoria Island. Who in spite of their acidic and bitchy gossip still clamored to be guests at her occasional dinners. For only those that really mattered were invited. Though they were seldom seen in public together it was understood by all that she was Mustapha's. A few months later he set her up in an apartment in Victoria Island, but she often still stayed at home in Ikoyi.

Her father was a little disappointed at the liaison, but he expected them to marry, which in reality was a distant hope. He insisted though that Mustie gave her a ring which he sent for, from New York, large diamond ring from Tiffany& Co. then her fingers too became a topic for gossip. All in all the Alhaji was not pleased, like all black men, his heart bled a little whenever he saw a black woman in the clutches of a white man . It is a deep rooted behavior that is based upon the premise that the best man always gets the woman and he saw it as though she was a prize for having invaded the country, especially as Mustie was rich. But it was also because he was rich that he condoned him. In the final analysis he would have preferred Mustapha to an Igbo or Yoruba from the south. But none had told him, for no one knew that Mustapha was hardly the best choice for his precious daughter whom he had bred so well.

TEN

SATURDAY *20TH APRIL* 1985

I

When Binta received a telephone message from Romano informing her that Mustapha had returned from his travels, she went to see him. As Mustapha was in a meeting in his study she decided to swim while she waited for the meeting to end. She swam lazily in the still pool. It was an insignificant day. She did her lengths, mechanically, hardly enjoying it, only for the exercise. She became obsessed with keeping in shape. It was part of her newly acquired vanity, the clothes and the fact that she had become a figure of social importance and envy, which put her on display and as such she made an effort to look her best, even now when was so unhappy.

Romano walked past her as she splashed in the pool without even acknowledging her presence. She didn't know if he liked her at all but she was wise enough not to cross swords with him in any way for she suspected, wrongly, that he had some influence over Mustapha. No one had. He went to the sitting room where he met a man. He walked back to Mustapha's study with a customs officer who plodded behind him. From the pool she looked at the uniformed man whose protruding stomach strained against the buttons of his shirt. She was aware that she had seen him before; his cherubic cheeks and ring adorned fingers struck a note of recognition in her. But she could not remember exactly where and when.

After the unexpected episode of the previous evening Mustapha had eventually rested, having had a warm bath, brandy and sleep. Romano, his efficient right arm, had made the reports to their friends in influential positions and Musa Ahmed's assistant at the Ministry of Defence had promised to take care of the injured driver who was sent to hospital where he had received initial treatment for broken ribs and concussion and lay convalescing in a room at an expensive private clinic.

II

In his study Mustapha instructed Akintola Noga, the customs officer, on his new scheme.

'Noga, I hope you understand how it will all work?' Mustapha asked as their discussions drew to a close.

'Yes, sah!' the man replied

Noga, like many others in important government departments, was on the payroll of Mustapha's organization. The meeting concerned arrangements for the clearing of, ostensibly, a shipment of machinery spares.

'Where is Musa?' Mustapha asked as he stood, not waiting for a reply and left the room and Romano to finalize all detailed and operational plans of payments, collections and signatures with the customs man. He went out across the pool and into the house. Binta was in the shower when Mustapha walked into bedroom suite. He sat in his bedroom, had a few generous gulps of malt whisky while he waited and for her finish. 'Oh' she said, as she came out in a terry robe. They hugged. He kissed her passionately, whispered in her ear and undressed.

In her mind it was mechanical, purely animal. She had lost all genuine interest in his body and his actions. She was unable to act in any convincing way. Even though she moaned and twisted theatrically she suspected that he felt that she derived nothing. He did. After he spent himself he lay on his back and thought about it for a while and changed his thoughts to his business. It was filed in his memory as a black mark against her. He always did that, slowly carrying poisonous thoughts in his mind and heart until he took action, often violent, in return for numerous deeds he felt had been committed against him. Akin's ghost appeared between them as the affair crumbled under the strain of recent events causing pain and numbness. She stirred a little as tears welled up in her eyes, she was still so sad. She held his hand and squeezed it a little.

'Why didn't you help Akin, Mustie?' she asked whispering into his ear unaware that he had found out about the affair between them. He looked surprised for a moment. He had not expected her to ask him directly.

'How could I have done anything?'

'But he did work for you at times; at least I thought he did, didn't he?'

'Yes he did, but there was more.'

'Such as…' She asked letting out a deep breath.

'I could do nothing…there was nothing to do…it was out of my hands…way, way beyond me'

'Nothing's beyond you…if you wanted to….'she said almost pleading for an explanation. She caught herself and realized that she must be careful not to seem too interested, but she had gone too far already.

'But there must have been a way…'She continued throwing away all caution. It was too late anyway for caution. She was driven by that driving and searching curiosity which belongs only to those who care and are bereaved and she had certainly cared a lot for Akin.

'Why can't you leave it alone...?' He said firmly 'Do you think I'll put myself and my business at risk because of one small meaningless shrimp?' He said with finality. The words made her shudder inside. What a heartless user Mustapha was, she thought.

'Who is the fat man from customs?' She asked changing the topic and trying to diffuse the palpable tension that had arisen between them.

'You mean Noga? ... that's Noga…our friend in customs...He's very helpful, I met his father when I came to this country...The elder Noga has since retired… so now we continue spreading the money to the whole family…from father to son…the game continues.' He answered.

She had a small feeling about this man Noga, she felt that he must have been part of Akins fall as she lay in Mustapha's now uncomfortable and uneasy arms, the events of the past few months came to her, overwhelming her, Noga, the firing squad and as she tried to unravel the web of subterfuge that enclosed the affair, she wondered how she had become a part of it all, a part of the sordid events that led to Akin's fall.

ELEVEN

LAGOS *22APRIL* 1985

9.00 a.m., the sun was already hot as Muna-Muna walked down the dusty street towards a busy road where he could catch a taxi. The sky was blue and the sunshine, its beauty all about, bathed the day. He walked past a Mallam selling cigarettes and sweets on a small wooden table. They both greeted each other; 'ya *ya Kasuwa*?' Muna-Muna asked enquiring about the day's business. '*Ah Oga Na gode Allah*' the Mallam replied smiling and showing off dark brown cola nut-stained teeth. In the air Muna-Muna could smell the aroma of cooking as he passed the eating house with a 'food is ready' sign displayed outside. He almost went in for a quick beer and some goat pepper soup but as he had an important appointment so he walked on, he came to the junction he saw yellow cabs zip past.

'Lagos... Eko!' he screamed and they touched their brakes, slowing down, in attempt to stop and then move on.

'Bugger you!' Muna-Muna muttered under his breath slightly incensed by the tease. His worn out brown safari jacket with frayed collar was already soaked in perspiration as he stood waiting for a taxi. His pot belly strained against the buttons of his jacket and his fat cheeks protruded under the tight cheap almost comical black plastic sunglasses giving him the look of a strange hoodlum. A taxi came to a halt just beyond him and he ran up to it.

'Na marina I dey go o!' he said, as he entered into the car, only managing to squeeze his large frame into the small Datsun.

'Na wa O' he said panting, 'I no know say taxi dey hard like this', as he wiped sweat from his face with the sleeve of his shirt.

It was an old and rusty taxi that jangled over the undulations in the road. There was noise all about them; the taxi driver was perpetually tapping his horn to the juju music that came over the radio, joining in the abuses hurled at one another by other road users for daredevil driving tricks and the noise of cars as they cut from lane to lane in a succession of close shaves Muna-Muna tried to relax a little as he squashed up a small boy who was seated beside him. He changed taxis at the Marina Lagos Island and went to the address in Ikoyi.

Binta looked at her desperate mask which was reflected in the mirror, she had slept fitfully as dreams of Akin had come to her in her valium-induced sleep. She undressed and stepped into an ice cold shower, waking up by this method was another habit she had acquired from Mustie. As a consequence of her father's material bequests she belonged to the ever growing idle rich of Nigeria. She had no proper occupation really.

She had taken an interest in painting and had done a stint at an art School in London hardly attending classes, choosing to spend her time at chic cafes and restaurants, visiting fashionable designer shops where she was often fobbed off with some of the rubbish that the designer world inflicted on the idle and rich. She was really a naive sort, having no real beliefs and waiting to be swayed by some forceful character or ideas. After she showered she had a glass of orange juice, went out into the garden and lounged beneath the blossoming flame-of-the forest tree, its blood red flowers filling the garden with a tropical color burst. She was dressed in a summery pastel-colored T-shirt and faded old jeans. She could not see the gold dust of sunlight sprinkled by God on the beautiful day. Her mind, numbed by bereavement, was still, and she stared at the garden and at the gardener as he trimmed the thick green hedge into large square shapes.

The morning heat affected her dazed mind and she tumbled into a quasi-sleep, a dreamy state in which she saw images of the sun, gleaming like a star right before her eyes. She did not hear the metallic clang as Muna-Muna slammed the door of the rickety taxi and the taxi driver screamed

'Oga you go pay if you spoil my motor o!' She did not hear him scrunch on the gravel drive as he walked in. She didn't notice him until he walked across the smooth lawn to the shade of the tree. She awoke when, she heard his voice.

'Muna-Muna' he said in a deep thick solemn voice. 'I am Muna-Muna... you remember from the note?' he repeated.

She stared at him, a little jolted and bewildered stirred from sleep.

She had expected him to be slim, perhaps very much like Akin and for a split second she wondered if Akin would, had he lived, have grown to be a fat man too one day.

'I am pleased' she said,' Very pleased to meet you' in her perfect English and she offered him her hand limply.

'Maybe a soft drink perhaps, it is a hot day?' she continued.

'Yes, I like minerals!' he said smiling enthusiastically and exposing his perfect white teeth. He paused a little.

'Maybe beer... I like beer pass minerals.' He continued smiling broadly.

She called to the gardener, ordered drinks for both of them from the house; soon Muna-Muna was comfortably seated on a cane chair with a glass of beer in his hand and cold cans before him.

'It's a bad thing that has happened in this our country.' Muna-Muna said sipping the beer in the most civilized way he could.

Binta watched him, tried to form an opinion of him from his face, his speech, and his gesticulations. But it was not so easy. For appearances were so often deceptive.

'You know I'm talking of Akin my nephew.' He said

'Yes I know you mean Akin,' she said gently.

'You know say I only find your name for the book, the address book. You are the only one, the only friend that I know he had.'

She listened to him but she was not about to share her grief with a stranger and even though she wanted a shoulder to cry on, it wouldn't be under a tree in the garden on the shoulder of a beer breathed fat man that she would cry.

'What do you want of Akin, why are you asking me?' She said as tears welled up in her eyes blurring her vision.

'You know I was not in Lagos...' Muna-Muna said he continued recounting his story.

'I was in Yola on posting and from there, posting, posting, posting everywhere then I hear that they have retired me. Na wa for this our life o!' He said grumbling.

'So tell me what you want.' Binta said.

'Yes… that's what I'm saying is this my nephew I know am. I know am well, well, right from the time wey them born am my eye dey for him head because him be my sister pikin. And I know say him be thief but him never reach the one of firing squad. Cocaine na lie...Akin no fit do that kind thing...From which place wey him learn that kind thing' he said flowing in Pidgin English.

'Oh really, what do I know, he's gone, he's gone. What difference does it make, Mr. Muna?'

'Not Mr., never Mr., I am Inspector Muna-Muna retired!' He said emphatically, raising his eye brows. The beer had charged him up a little.

'I'm sorry.' She said apologetically.

'Wetin you bin wan say?' he asked satisfied that he had established himself.

A little silence passed as he had, by his interruption taken the words from her mouth. He watched her through his dark sunglasses. He also tried to assess her. Having been in the police force for over twenty years he acquired a certain understanding of people. He looked at her dark eyes and they softened him. He liked her. In her beauty the smoldering fires of his youthful virility were rekindled. And he felt a little pain in his heart; such a nice girl should have to bear the loss of a close friend. He could tell that she was good, she was a good girl He could feel it. There was hardly any evil in her. He took another large swig of his drink and continued to think about her.

Binta still struggled to hold back her tears and keep it all together. Her vision was clouded with tears but still she tried her best to appear indifferent. It was an unwritten code of her Anglo Saxon upbringing that one never bared one's soul to strangers, she thought as she tried to put her chin up and look dignified. He had broken the weak scab from a slightly healed wound and she bled. Akin had come to matter to her though she knew that there was little that lasted forever, she had hoped they would have had a little more time.

'I know say na people wey dey help am do this thing him been dey do' Muna-Muna said breaking the silence.

'What do you mean?' She replied.

'You know wetin I mean him no been day alone...' He said with certainty in his voice.

Binta said nothing. She knew what he was driving at, he believed that Akin had not acted alone and was part of a grand crime gang. It was exactly what she had suspected deep in her heart. It scared her just in case her Mustie was involved. She stared at him. He had a kind face and the fact that he was Akins's uncle made her like him. He was a little rustic, but he had no evil in him even though he seemed a right drunkard. She knew that Mustapha would eat him for breakfast, it was best to feign total ignorance and not encourage his suicide, for that is what it would be, pure suicide for him to try to delve into the affairs of Mustapha and Romano.

'Abi you no 'gree Wetin I talk?' He said

'What?' she replied having let her mind wander off for a moment?

'You no 'gree say there must be people wey dey behind dis cocaine matta?' He continued trying to probe her.

'What does it matter, let the dead man alone, let him sleep peacefully in God's bosom' She replied

'How can?! Na my pickin... if I no fight for am na who go stand up for him... You know say poor man no get brother, you no see as rich men, Government de take poor man like say him be nothing... I must find out show them say not all of us be fools.' He said. Binta stood; she could no longer fight her tears.

'Muna-Muna... so sorry inspector Muna retired. ...I have places to go and much to do so I must take my leave of...' she turned one walked dragging her feet across the lawn. A gentle breeze moved the warm heat about but the sun still burned down. And when she walked into the red brick building she found it was much cooler inside.

'You go help me... you must help me!' Muna-Muna pleaded adamantly from the garden.

She knew he would be back; he seemed a determined type that would doggedly continue to pursue Mustapha. It would be better to keep silent. She could taste salt in her mouth as she wiped her tears away with her palms.

TWELVE

I

The pursuit of power corrupts absolutely. Mustapha, like most men who have amassed wealth, sought to crown it with political power. He did not want to ask for favors with financial gratitude tied to them, he wanted to be a power broker.

Political stability has so far, unfortunately become a privilege of the West. Underprivileged black Africa has so far suffered painful instability. Theirs has been a history of extreme political and social unrest over the past few decades. Especially countries that have been 'cursed' by the presence of substantial commercial oil reserves, the exploitation of which at one time bestowed instant wealth has now become a tale of sorrow, for the wealth which brought abundance, has left sorrow and poverty, the changing fortunes of the oil industry worldwide has turned the tables from plenty to scarcity. There is no longer money to burn, the country has, almost, been posted for sale there are still men like Mustapha who are able to use her a stepping stone to unimaginable illicit and immoral wealth. Corruption in negotiations that involve power and money has been the carrot that has guaranteed success to his kind. Mustapha believed, a little naively that by financing the efforts of some mercenary, power hungry soldier he could purify his wealth. He thought that he would no longer need to hide away from the world and the press, if he could finance a government into power. He assumed that he would be looked upon with respect by the new Government and also the world. He wanted to achieve in less than a generation that respectability that is commanded by *old money* after it has been handed down from father to son in the cleansing process of generational inheritance. He sought all of this because he had come to the zenith for a man in his position. He wanted to feature as a respected businessman, on *Fortune* magazine's lists and to become an international figure in acceptable society. This he sought to do through Musa Ahmed, whom he had secretly and quietly cultivated for several years. He had earlier recognized ambition in Musa Ahmed, and he had also noticed and noted, more importantly, Musa's cunning and guile. He was convinced that Musa was equipped to mastermind a takeover plot. As such, Mustapha was prepared to finance him. He was willing to risk money; it would be worth the risk, for if Musa succeeded, Mustapha would be the most powerful man in Nigeria, maybe even in all of Africa.

It had been arranged, as a sort of guarantee to Mustapha, that he would have nothing to do with the details so that he would not be able, even if he wanted to, to trade information with anyone. Mustapha did not really want to know the details as he was only interested in the end result. It was Musa's first victory though, for he had been responsible for manipulating the arrangements so that Mustapha could merely provide the money, he did not trust anyone and as such preferred to be in total control of the situation.

II

22nd APRIL 1985

In his study in Victoria Island, Mustapha sat, the crowded bookshelves behind him, gazing out of the large glass sliding doors at the pool, which like a mirror reflected and cross-reflected infinite images. He was cool; the efficient air conditioners chilled and de-humidified his surroundings. It was early afternoon, a warm day, yellow sunshine and dark shadows. It was almost the warmest time of the year before the rains came. Romano knocked on the carved ebony door of his study and ushered Musa Ahmed in. Musa walked in with his usual deliberate gait, dressed in a white brocade *babariga* and dark sunglasses which he seldom removed from his face. His Fingers were adorned with gaudy gold, diamond silver jewels which he mixed, indiscriminately and ignorantly in a repulsive clash.

'Ah… Musa Ahmed' Mustapha said waving him to come and sit opposite him   'Where were you when we needed you?' He continued. Musa bowed and sat. 'Yes, yes. I heard…Allah be praised.' He replied 'How was London?' He asked.

'It was fine.' Mustapha replied

'I heard of it all; No more Ben…eh?' He asked. Mustapha shook his head solemnly

'No more....' Mustapha replied grimly and nodded to Romano who was standing beside the door as an indication that he should leave them, he left the room. Musa and Mustapha spoke softly as though words were rare and were to be frugally expended. But they were fully aware, from the look of seriousness on their faces that this was a delicate matter.

'I have been notified of the arrangements and the bank has let me know that there is money.'

'What did you receive?' Mustapha asked.

I received three, plus the previous two that I transferred.... That is five now' Musa responded.

'Then I wash my hands of you, for now.' Mustapha said, gesticulating like Pilate.

'Have you begun to make your arrangements?'

'Don't fail me or you shall find me difficult. If you need protection, if anything goes wrong, you may go to Columbia, no one can touch you there.' Mustapha said.

'Can't fail', Musa said stiffly. '...I am yet to fail at anything.' he continued

'But there is always a first time.' Mustapha said wryly. 'Have a cigar, relax.' He continued.'

'There is always a first time...' He was smiling. Musa smoked.

'Do you want something to drink? Some wine?, whiskey? Anything...'Mustapha asked

'You have Lanson?'Musa enquired.

'I wouldn't mind some Chamfagne,' He continued

'Good, I will join you, I like champagne too'. They both drank and puffed on large cigars that seemed choke them.

'There is plenty to be happy for, at least now the heat will be off us.....' Mustapha said.

'After the execution before I left; I hear that I'm almost a hero in military circles' Musa said.

'There was so much trouble, so much trouble with the authorities at the airport' Mustapha said.

'At least it can take all the attention away from me...' Musa Ahmed observed

'Congratulations are in order don't you think?'

'Yes. We made sure that he had so much on him that he looked like more than a mere runner.'

'Yes, they all thought that he was a baron himself...' Mustapha said.

They filled their glasses, celebrating the execution that they had been responsible for.

'Will that be all?' Musa asked his glass on the table. 'I must leave to attend to something urgent.'

'Only that you must tell me in advance generally when you will move so that I can be away from here in case things get rough.' Mustapha said with an air of added seriousness in his voice.

Mustapha stood, the meeting was over and Musa stood too.

'Good luck.' Mustapha said offering him his hand. Romano escorted Musa Ahmed out of the building. The sun and shadows played hide and seek in the tranquil tropical garden outside as evening came. And in Musa was born treason, a toddler who walked towards the throne, guided by the shylock Mustapha. Mustapha poured himself some more bubbly. He could feel the birth of a new order, a new energy flowed through him and it would soon flow through the land. He went to his desk, opened a silver desk-top vial and sniffed a little of the white powder sharply through each nostril, and he celebrated his impending rise to the corridors of legitimate power.

THIRTEEN

5.30 p.m. Monday *22nd April,* 1985

Muna-Muna slumped into the chair in his parlor, dead tired. He was exhausted but it had been an interesting day, he thought, remembering his meeting with Binta. He had already made his mind up about her; even though she had been cold to him he knew that there was still a way. As an old policeman he was aware that on the first questioning the subject was bound to be withdrawn. A fly buzzed in the hot and humid little sitting room of his dwelling as the fading daylight came in through the small louvered windows.

'Kofo!' he shouted, 'way de *eba* now? ... Eh dis woman abi you no want make I chop?' He stood, still muttering under his breath and walked into the bedroom, where he removed his jacket and shirt displaying his rounded belly. He was sober, as the morning's beer had long since ceased to affect him, and to him that brought on melancholy. He craved for more of the sweet brew; at least it would quell his sobriety, a state in which he saw the world for what it was a vulgar and difficult temporary home.

More than anything he hated to accept and admit that he was a failure. He looked around his squalid rooms and it was clear to him, blindingly clear that he had not done well for himself. After twenty-nine years in the police force he had retired to penury and insignificance. He had been an inspector for ten years and he had been given the worst postings. He was often to be found on the peripheral police stations in the lifeless backwaters of the sprawling nation. He had paid the price for honesty, poverty.

A fungal mustiness hung still in the humidity of the bedroom as there was no cross ventilation, hardly any ventilation at all, as the window of the room opened to a high wall, which was often wet and obliterated even the light from the bedroom. Muna-Muna breathed with difficulty as he perspired and wandered back to the sitting room. He hated living in the tenement yard, with the little babies crying at night and the other families fighting and quarreling at odd hours. He could barely make use of the septic latrine, which was no more than a hole in the floor, when he wanted to. He was a broken man, living on the edge of sanity, trying in spite of all his frustrations to live a useful life. So why shouldn't he drink beer, the sanity saving brew, why? He had every reason in the world to suck down as much of it as he could.

His wife Kofo had already placed on a small tables his *gari* and watery *egusi* soup. He washed his hands in a basin of water and quickly settled down to swallow the hot *eba*. And how much had he gained from this country? He asked himself. This was the country to which he had given the best years of his life in service as a policeman. He was infuriated, like a betrayed wife, having been dealt a poor hand in a card game of high stakes. Someone would have to pay, he thought; if he could get his hands on any of the past leaders he would wring their necks with relish. He ate quickly and soon emptied the bowl of *gari* then he finished the soup, polished off the meat and munched the bones.

'Beer!' he yelled. '…If man no fit drink then na wetin him de wait, make him die!' he said loudly.

He licked his fingers and washed them and as soon as Kofo settled the bottle of beer before him, he emptied it.

The food had finally broken him and he plodded to his bedroom and lay on the wobbling bed. He would not give up, he would pursue his investigations. Evening slowly faded in, as darkness engulfed his world. He slept, forgetting his plight and delivered his mind to his dreams.

FOURTEEN

6.00PM *MONDAY 22nd APRIL* 1985

She smoked in solitude. After Muna-Muna had left, she had climbed to her favorite place, the extended flat concrete roof of the kitchen that abutted the red brick colonial house. There she let the grey tobacco smoke flow from her lips into the air. Evening drew close and she lay on her back with her feet touching the parapet. As her eyes searched the slowly darkening sky, she wondered what lay in the vast space beyond. She puffed in silence and thought about her world, her volatile existence. Her mind floated back to vivid memories of those wood-paneled, cool corridors of her Alma Mater. Back to the shingled beach of the Sussex Coast, the languid seemingly never ending summers, bluebells in the woods, picnics in golden sunshine moistened by the dew of sweet, almost heavenly, red, white and bubbling wines. And back to cold winters that had forged her spirit. She remembered it all. Vividly, she considered for a moment, the present which had in those days been distant, unpredictable and mysterious. She was, somehow disappointed with the present, as is always the case, for she had envisaged a different condition. A more gentle and settled present, a marriage to a respectable and powerful meteoric rising star of the Northern elite, a lovely family with beautiful babies, but she had never been one to force the future, allowing life to take its own course. She didn't twist the hand of fate, for she believed that it was all written, predestined.

Binta had grown up alone. A black face in a white world, by her education understanding their ways as though she was one of them but being, at the same time, ever conscious of the fact that she would never belong, entirely. She was, by her upbringing, in a perpetual state of limbo. On her return home, she had found herself unprepared for life in the unique and wonderful turbulent African country. All in all, she was a misfit, a flexible one at that, but a misfit all the same.

She had tried, like most do when faced with difficult problems, to push them to the back of her mind, to forget them and pretend that they were nonexistent. It was difficult, though, for the ghosts would always return like a nightmare to haunt her conscience. She had suspected all along that there must have been some plot, some reason to explain his death. She refused to believe that he had been caught just like that. Today, when the fat man came to her, he had aroused her suspicions. He had set her thinking, on the inevitable course, that

Mustie was part of Akin's death. It was something that she, for fear, had refused to contemplate. She was a coward and it was also because she was afraid, that she was under Mustapha's complete control. The evening birds, coming out, chirped and hopped on trees and on the lawn in the green garden. She was a receptive person, who felt things, both physical and spiritual but sometimes she was lost between the two. This caused Akin's death to seem unrealistic. In her grief, her suppressed emotions of bereavement, she had questioned the authenticity of his death. Was it so simple, she wondered? That she could feel him and touch him, she could be consoled by his physical person, feel the love of his spirit and his companionship and then suddenly have him disappear into nothingness. Exit in vacuous death. It was hard to believe. But now Muna-Muna had opened her eyes to the existence of another reality, she began to accept it, the possibility of his having been set up and executed. And pain fathered bitterness and hate. She contemplated some sort of vengeance there on the concrete roof. In the short tropical twilight as the trees, once green in daylight, became black silhouettes in the fading light of the descending sun, she somehow saw with the ex-policeman that someone must pay.

But that was not the half of it. Binta had much more on her mind. She was at an age when she had acquired that middle maturity which is a feminine gem. She was of the age when unmarried women seem to grasp and hold fervently to whatever relationship comes their way. Maybe that was what made Akin so important to her. But it was not all of it. She touched her body, her breasts and stomach in a seemingly erotic light-fingered touch as she mused. She had something that none would take from her. She had told no one that she held some part of him. He would live again when the baby was born, and she smiled, in victory over death, a victory that even Mustapha with all his worldly powers would be able to take from her, she had not been entirely cheated. She puffed on what was left of the tasteless cigarette and made a mental note to quit the smoking habit very soon for the sake of the baby, as she looked up at distant stars that twinkled in constellation, at the darkening sky and at God in his Heavens, the omnipresent eyes that lighted the world and she wondered, as she had done years ago at school. What other nefarious surprises would spring on her from Pandora's Box.

FIFTEEN

WEDNESDAY *24th APRIL* 1985

He had taken ill the previous night. Mustapha lay in a warm, almost hot semi-sleep. His white bedroom was still and the ornamental ceiling fan twirled, fanning him with the warm afternoon air. He could taste the bitter camoquine on his tongue and his bones, joints and muscles ached as malaria pummeled him. He was weak. Beside him on the side table was a half empty jug of fresh orange juice. He hated being ill; and then he hated Nigeria, the disease, the humidity. He felt itchy all over, scratching himself all over, attempting to locate the source of the itch.

'Damn it,' he said 'Damn the camoquine and malaria!' He continued. He looked out to the marble floored patio beside his bedroom at the potted palms, winding evergreen creepers and the purple blossom of bougainvillea in the yellow afternoon. There, darting in spastic movements was a dragonfly; sometimes it flew over the sick man and then out again into the daylight. He lay, his head on the soft feather pillow, gazing. His mind too was weak but he kept on thinking. Sometimes losing the order of his thoughts and seeing snippets; images of his ideas. He had almost lost all his senses of direction. The burning ambition that had driven him to achieve had waned. It was no longer spurred by the inward desire to make one all-powerful and respected, but his actions-those of his organization-were acts of habit, almost.

In all this time, this history of ascent, his sanity had been eroded. His conscience had become a tally card of countless destructive achievements. He had lost control of his mind. It had grown, warped and disorderly, into a monster with no master. His subconscious, the id, spurned demons that would perpetually haunt him. He shook, sweating in feverish tremble, as his mind again conjured up vivid pictures of the past images of blood stained corpses of men and women, murdered lovers, accomplices, enemies and friends. He opened his eyes in confusion seeing the face he had set eyes on only once, the dark smooth face of Akin. It zoomed up at him, as though on film, and haunted him. He tossed, sat up in aching movement and looked to the door. It opened and Romano walked in, small and stocky, his pistol bulging in its sheath beneath his armpit.

'Is she here?' Mustapha asked weakly.

'She's coming soon, I have sent for her... She should be here anytime soon' Romano said in reply.

Romano walked across the room to the balcony where he sat before a chess table and examined carefully the hand-crafted glass and malachite pieces. Mustapha's eyes followed his every move, seeing not only his person but his aura. Through his aching eyes he looked at Romano. He considered him to be his longstanding lackey, almost a eunuch. He parted his lips to speak to him. To tell him of his fear, his confusion, his powerful mind. But he stopped, as he usually did, whenever he was close to revealing any real truth about himself. He did not trust people and as such was reluctant to allow the true Mustapha to be touched; this habitual concealment caused the good and better part of him, to recede further into the wells of his heart, to an unreachable place. And many doubted that there was any good left in him at all. He was lost in himself, confused and eroded by a constantly hardening and overbearing evil streak. It had all come to a head now and the fever untied the knots of the sanity that held him together.

He saw Romano, after all these years, as a dangerous ally, only to be used and not to be confided in. He thought of her and waited for her. He knew that he had felt something for her at some stage, at the birth of the affair. But that feeling too, like all good feelings of his, had been subdued by his dark side, driven into hiding in the unreachable recesses of his mind. He wasn't sure that he still felt anything for her. Not after what she had done to him. Not after Akin. But he had to keep her with him, at least until there was another. If there would ever be any that could touch that hard stone of his; his twisted heart. He lost the battle to keep awake and closed his eyelids, opening the gates of his warped mind and setting free demons from his past. Romano sat on the patio watching over him, an armed angel. Mustapha had sent for her and she came quickly. She had been rushed over in the Mercedes, it was clear that she was still at his back and call. As Binta walked into the white bedroom towards his bed she was aware that these were the last days of her affair with Mustapha.

She could feel, as her female intuition pricked her that their affair had come to its end. She only wondered how it would finally end. For she could not see them sliding peacefully apart Nothing about Mustapha or his life was at all peaceful. She put up a smiling face, said hello to Romano and sat beside Mustapha.

Mustapha had fallen asleep and didn't realize that she had come and was there but she stayed a little while holding his hand and wiping perspiration from his forehead with a cool damp towel press. She still felt a little fondness for him, maybe for the past, for her ignorant and inexperienced past. She was like that, caring too much for people, even for her enemies. She had stayed enough and made her mind to go downstairs to look at the flowers blossoming in the garden as Romano spoke.

'It's hot.' Romano said to her, wiping his face with a handkerchief.

'Rather…' she replied. 'No air conditioning?'

'None,' Romano said. 'The doctor, he said not to put it on'.

'Oh' she said, standing up.

'Will he be well soon?' She asked.

'Well I'll go downstairs and sit out… it's much cooler there…' She continued

'I wish I could come with you' Romano said 'but I have to be here, you understand.'

She smoothed her white linen dress, turned and walked to the door.

'I say…' she said… turning at the door 'Is there any chance of my seeing the customs man?' A friend, a girlfriend wants a car in from the ports'

'You mean Akintola Noga?' Romano asked.

'Yes' Binta said

'Yes… no problem…I will send him to you at home.' He said.

'Thanks.' Binta said with a little smile. She closed the door behind her and walked away from the room, her stilettos tapping sharply on the polished grey marble floor as she walked down the long corridor.

SIXTEEN

Friday *26th April* 1985.

Grey day. A misty haze hung foggily in the morning, obscuring the sunlight. The air was cool and Musa Ahmed could see through his binoculars the black passing images against the grey sky, floating feathered observers. He was dressed in mufti, his usual garb, and could hear the sound of close by traffic, non-stop taxi horns and the throb of big truck engines going past. He sat up in the pavilion and observed unnoticed, the parade of guards in the ceremonial square that once used to be a racecourse He was armed as usual and his pistol was tucked behind his belt, ready for almost any eventuality. As he watched the khaki clad automatons jerking robotically in crisp military drill, a gush of sentimentality came over him. His heart somehow was in the unreal display of his profession, for he was truly a soldier at heart. He always wanted to be a part of the important affairs of his country and the only way in which he could ever have achieved this was through the army. He broke a kola nut and put half of it into his mouth chewing quickly, crunching the bitter caffeine-laden rust colored fruit. He felt his pockets for his Marlboros, took one out, lit it and smoked. The grey smoke blended perfectly with the dull day. He took out a pen and a small white pad and scribbled coded notes quickly; when he had finished, he looked out again through the binoculars at the events below him. The guards had stopped marching now and stood to attention for inspection. A young officer, well built, fair, with a clean shaven face walked slowly on polished brown shoes with his swagger stick under his arm, inspecting the guard. Musa nodded his head, 'that's him' he said to himself in Hausa. He put down the binoculars and wrote more, a smile appeared on his face and he looked down again at the officer. '*Yana da kyau*,' he said to himself. It meant very stylish.' He was preoccupied with style and visual impressions. Musa had been part of many coup plots. In fact, it was rumored that any plot without him was bound to fail. It was not because he had always wanted to be on the good side of government but because he had to guarantee his future, his promotion, his rising army career. It was so easy to lose one's place. The successful plotters did not forget a friend more than they remembered well those that had initially refused the hand of friendship. Musa was too smart for that and as such, he was everyone's friend. This made him lonely.

It was inevitable that one day he would try to seize government himself; he had acquired the practical experience in a dangerous field.

He could see that the execution of this particular plot would be more complex than the previous ones for there was less central power in this government. There was more than one strong arm man and he would have to diffuse each of them separately. The easiest way of doing this would be by pitting them against each other. The sun, still slightly shrouded, was winning its waking battle and her dulled rays warmed him. Musa relaxed, not instantly wanting to go to his office at the Independence Building he let his mind ponder about it all. He saw himself as very intelligent. And indeed he was. But his vanity reduced his capabilities somewhat. He had previously made the mistake of underestimating his opponents. Like most intelligent people, he was condescending in thought and was consequently an introverted snob. He thought of the distant past, during the civil war. He remembered best the early days of action when they had marched, almost without hindrance, through Ogoja. After a short battle experience he was moved back to headquarters in Lagos and worked on propaganda. It was from there that he began intelligence work; assessing the trend of the hostilities, how much truth to let out to the foreign press and how to advice his superiors; how much to tell them and how much to keep to himself. He was quick to note that even in the army; brawn was not the key asset.

He slowly took care to personally investigate all his colleagues and sometimes, when necessary, he would use his secret reserves of information on them to help secure his promotions and postings over his fellow officers. This wand of threatened disclosure often did the trick. He usually got what he wanted. He was married once, out of conformity, as most young army officers do once commissioned. He learnt that blackmail was dangerous when his Fulani wife and driver died mysteriously in a motor accident crushed between two Lorries on the death trap of a road between Zaria and Kaduna. It had made him vengeful, fuelled his ambition and made him want more; even for a man who played intrigue easily he was unable to find those responsible for the death of his wife, especially since he had been the target of the 'accident'. That was in 1971 after the civil war. It had touched him, not because he loved her, he did not, but because he realized for the first time the real dangers of his work. He was more careful after that incident and took pains to practice his shooting often. He smoked another cigarette, the fumes of his thoughts. As the parade closed the sergeant major ordered them to march away crisply and dust was raised by the boots. The sun had won, and Musa wiped beads of perspiration from his forehead with his handkerchief. Its unimpaired rays of golden heat were scorching.

He thought now of the future as he stood up and walked down the stairs, he had come a long way, alone for the past odd decade, his son, Musa too, was at a Military School in the United States. He could afford things like that now. He was always well dressed in well-cut suits and expensive brocade.

He usually wore exquisite jewels, which were at times almost feminine, but that was his prerogative, apart from his dress and taste for fine wines he was hardly opulent. He had no personal car and his personal house was a small bungalow up north, it was impossible to tell that he had earned millions of United States dollars in commissions on a defense contract and that he had made much more than that from helping Mustapha by giving him military intelligence cover and information for his activities. He was, all in all, a miser, like most obsessed with money, he never used a kobo of his own money to further his arrangements. He was too smart for that; he had the sense to use Mustapha's largesse. He walked quickly for a man of forty seven, like an adolescent marching into life, towards his car. Care, he thought, we must pick our men with care. It was almost twelve noon and he went home to prepare for his prayers.

SEVENTEEN

Friday 26ᵗʰ April **1985**

He sat, drinking beer, in the afternoon heat on the verandah at Madam Calabar's eating house. Muna-Muna had not done anything for the past few days; he was still in lazy retirement. The sun's yellow rays shone on the land; illuminating rising dust from the red dirt road, drying septic green gutters that lay exposed on the roadside. He sipped his Star beer, as he sat, leaning precariously on the tottering wooden chair.

'Madame O!' he shouted his gruff voice bellowing in the cool dark bar. She came out swinging her generous hips nimbly between the tables and chairs   'Bring me annoder biar and Congo meat' he commanded ordering another beer and peppered snails. His voice was rather loud, he was not really a loud man it was just the way of his people. They were more physical, earthy, as they lived fully in a physical world where life itself was ample, abundant, not as it was in the temperate zones of the world where life had that spiritual and civilized chill but the throbbing flesh that danced and drank and sang to earthy almost gross tempos of tropical madness. He was just black that was it, he was his own person; African.

He slid further down the beer-sodden trail into mild tranquility. The people passed him as they paced the overcrowded street in search of direction, in search of a slice of modern Africa; a misnomer for that mixed up, destabilized continent that hung swaying on the tight rope between the traditional and Western civilization. Most of them were Idle. Lost somewhat, like Muna-Muna in a system they knew nothing about. They were sub-pawns in a chess game of political wrangling. Muna-Muna was not concerned. He was in many ways a contented drunk, a nice drunk. It should not be imagined that all drunks are obstreperous and staggering; sometimes they are rather quiet and well behaved in their drunkenness. Somehow, he had not contacted her for days even though he had vowed to. Delay was part of his plan; he would give her time to think it over. And then he would have to squeeze the information out of her for he wasn't at all convinced. He knew that she was keeping something away from him. After all, he had been a 'force man'.

Madame Calabar brought him peppered snails in stew and another bottle of beer and he smacked his lips.

'Dis Madame, you too dey like me o!' he said, subdued by the food and drink.

He had never been an ambitious man, only himself. His needs were simple: to live in peace. He was not burned by desire to over achieve, to better himself and to break records of any sort, he was contented simply coasting along and making up the numbers as long as he could have a few cold beers once in a while. He was a safe human. Safe because disruption, acrimony and jealousy are the consequences of intelligence which often manifests as unbridled personal ambition and greed. All of which can culminate in megalomania and a Hitler-like desire to 'rule the world.' He had been happy, sort of, with his wife Kofo, in the police force, taking the odd 'dash' here and there and never faltering from the beer. But his forced retirement, the conviction and execution of his nephew had shaken him from his blissful ignorance and awoken him to the harsh realities of his condition. He was angry and he contemplated a million ways to get even. He was convinced that the only way Akin could have been caught up in the whole drug smuggling system was through someone. He would go back to her, talk some sense to her and shake her up a bit. She was a fine girl, too *onyibo*, but fine. She would talk; eventually.

EIGHTEEN

NEW YEARS EVE 1984-MUSTAPHA'S PARTY

I

In the warm night the angular white building glistened in the moonlight. There was music, sweet lilting jazz that pervaded the house, the garden, the minds of the guests, and with the alcohol, made them feel relaxed. This was the party of the man who had everything. Everyone, as it is said, 'who was anyone' in Lagos was present. There was, beside the lighted swimming pool close to the gazebo, a bar. It was almost all made of glass; amid the twinkling glass, there stood a graying barman who mixed red, yellow, and clear waters, spirits and juices into potent cocktails. Beautiful girls, clad in silk, chiffon and dazzling sequins stood, propped up by the bar and drank fizzy wines from tall stemmed crystal flutes. Mustapha stood, Romano behind him, not far from the bar and shook hands with his guests and mixed with them. The New Year's Eve party had become his annual show; he had to remind the elite that he was still in Lagos. That he could still be relied on and that they should rely on him.

Alone at a table, the smooth Musa Ahmed sat dressed in a white breezy suit sipping sour bubbly, as always, in his dreamy state. Across, a young man stood alone, not feeling at all comfortable, watching Musa, his eyes burning with hate as his mind recalled the physically humiliating, sexually debasing and animalistic primal initiation rites he had suffered at Musa's hands. He had already made much financial progress in his illegal activities and had taken to attending several similar functions that were frequently held by the rich of the city. Akin swayed a little in the night breeze, high on cocaine as his eyes glistened. In the pool, girls splashed about in the sun-warmed waters as the band softly played Cole Porter's '*Sentimental Journey*.' Mustapha's residence was soaked, more than usual, in opulence. Akin's brown eyes searched the party for an interesting face, something with character. He passed over the beautiful and boring girls that were abundant. He lit a cigar (he had recently taken to them) and puffed, ignorantly inhaling the tar-laden smoke. He would circulate, he thought; mix with the crowd for what it was worth. '*Hell…*' he said to himself '*a man's got only one life to live…so live it I say!*'

Binta, delectable as ever, was also present at the party. She walked towards the pool house in a classic evening dress. She was, this evening especially, a goddess among men. She too, like most of the guests at the party, in these early hours of the function had already over-indulged in alcohol and was feeling a definite 'buzz' She walked to a small wooden bench beside the shower cabinet in the pool house and sat. It was 11.30 p.m., only thirty minutes remained of the year. She looked at her watch steadily, trying to focus her intoxicated eyes and read the time. '*Ah, almost time*' she said to herself thinking aloud, she thought and she could feel the sharp drop from her state of euphoria. The alcohol now made her feel depressed. She opened her gold sequin-encrusted hand bag and brought out a slim cigarette case from which she took a rolie laced with coca paste, Mustie had taught her quite well how to easily overcome depression; she lit it and smoked slowly as it held her and lifted her, injecting her mind with new energy; Sweetness. She smiled almost automatically as the feeling of elation came about her. She was, thanks to Mustapha, becoming a drug addict.

For once Romano, the semi statue, broke the mould of his casting and had a drink. He had several *Southern Comforts* as he never touched wine of any kind. He knocked back several jiggers and his belly was warm. But he stayed alert and still he had his pistol snuggly resting in its holster, ready for use. He and the other security staff were always prepared. There was a man on the roof and another one looked over the grounds from a window in the building, five men were in the party mixing freely with the guests, all armed and kept their eyes peeled. Rob Bungham, his sun bleached blonde hair hanging over his tanned skin sat at a table with a beauty drinking a pitcher of Millers' and talking glibly. He too was ready, at the shortest notice, to take the helicopter and Mustie away. It was a mixture of all kinds of people there; some, ambassadors, followed closely by their perpetually smiling wives, as they made polite conversation with *agbada* and *babariga*-adorned business men who drank countless cold beers. There were young lawyers, famous local sportsmen and a few groups of musicians, local actors, newsmen, party addicts, gigolos and a general sprinkling of dressed up party freeloaders, there were even distinguished tourists visiting the country and many of those over-dressed sybaritic university girls that chased parties. The sky was clear and a silver crescent moon hung in an arc against a starry sky. Binta walked away from the pool house, lay on a wooden garden bench and looked to the sky. Quite coincidentally, as if her mind had been read, as she looked upwards towards the twinkling gems that are stars the band played Ian Carmichael's *'Stardust.'*

It made her cry. She lay lost in herself and the emotions that had grown with her recent past burst as the floodgates of her watershed broke, releasing a brine cascade. She was now confused, her thoughts of the party, her love, her recent feelings of cultural schizophrenia were brought to the top; Boiling. She resorted to her new refuge and this time did not smoke it but with the aid of a small silver spoon she snorted the white powder which she had taken from a silver-encrusted box in her bag. It was then that he came to her.

I

Akin had, on account of his new wealth, acquired certain arrogance. It was much like the arrogance of the noveau riche, the 'instant feeling of importance' with which they are plagued. He was, when all was taken into account, still quite a nice person. But his conversation, which had never been laudable, had deteriorated to self proclaiming syntax and as such was misleading. He had no friends and the only women he knew were bedmates. He hardly had any regrets though, at least not yet, for he had received the dreams that he had bargained for. He had after a few trips for Musa made enough money to have all that he wanted as a young man. He had girls and alcohol, sex and more sex, speed and more speed in his new fuel injected sports BMW. He thought, in his empty childish manner, that there was nothing more that he could ask for. The future, by virtue of being unexpected and mysterious has always surprised those on which it wreaked its store. Akin was no exception. He might, if he had been given the chance to see his future before he was born, have decided not to have lived at all. The New Year came, just like midnight on every other day, the merry makers cheered and kissed one another. Akin was, like most mortals, unaware of his fate in the New Year and as he was still high walked slowly on the soft rolled lawn away from the party towards a garden bench. The he saw her. Through the dull vision of her glazed eyes she saw him, tall, fresh and fine, as he approached her. She sat up.

'Hey Babes…' Akin said still sporting his contrived accent.

'I just found me a pretty baby,' he continued trying to sound American. She stared plain faced at him.

'I will sit down...' he said squeezing beside her. There was a little silence between them and she stared in front of her at the party.

'Happy New Years!' he said trying to sound cheerful. She was still silent

'Will, will... get you a drink,' he said stuttering a little.

'That's nice,' she whispered. He hurried off and returned with two drinks.

'What's this?' she asked.

'This is old fashioned baby, old fashioned you know it?' he said smiling broadly.

'I'm Akin, the most beautiful... so are you' He said

'Oh' she said coldly.

He tipped his head back and finished the drink.

'Come on girl' he said 'do I smell or something?' He said

At that she laughed. She found him amusing.

'Not too much' she said replied smiling

'Your, your...your name...what's your name?' He said still stuttering.

'What certainly is not my name...'she said giggling 'it's Binta, just joking ...' She was feeling quite relaxed now, maybe it was the drink, the drugs, or maybe the evening or it may be even him. She was surprised with herself at the ease with which she allowed herself to be chatted up by him. There she was right there in Mustapha's house at his party! Thankfully they were out of sight. Unknowingly she was ripe to betray Mustapha and drift out of the relationship. She was ripe for another affair.

'Binta' she repeated, this time she stretched out her hand. Surprisingly Akin kissed it, it was something he had seen in the movies, and then he gave her a little bow, just like in the movies.

'Binta...That's real pretty' he said 'Akin at your service....' he said bowing down once more, more movie pretense. He had his best smile on his face as he put on the show for her.

'And what difference does that make?' she replied smiling on account of his compliment.

'It makes all the difference... babes... all the difference!'He said emphatically.

In the background there was still music in the night and the others danced. She turned towards Akin and looked at him, him at her. She saw beauty but he saw her eyes. The eyes are the gateway to the heart, they tell all, in those brown eyes he could read her, read those indelible events that had forged her spirit and he could, more than anything at that particular time tell that she warmed him and that she, if anyone, could be his salvation. She saw youth. She could tell, for she was a little wise, that he was not like her. That, in spite of all his efforts to appear prosperous, he was lost. He was like Mustapha, lost in luxury. She by her exposure and education was not so easily impressed by what she could not afford. But there was in him, something of what Mustapha had lost through age. The fiery animal of youth burnt through him and to her. She looked away, and so did he, as if both of them felt in their bones a twinge of the future. She covered her engagement ring and furtively slipped it onto another finger.

'What do you do?' she asked, unconsciously sizing him up.

'I am in business, you know Import/Export... big business' He said trying to impress her and convince himself that he was involved in an activity he could tell other people about. She knew that he was lying; she had hoped that he would be a rich man's son. That could be condoned.

'That's good' she replied 'I'm an artist' she continued.

'So... you play music/babe?' he asked.

'No. Not that…I'm a proper artist…I paint and write poems' She replied stuffily.

'What's a proper artist?' he asked

'I'm a painter, I paint. I like to paint the world in the way I see it.'

He could hardly understand her. She was odd, he thought, in his dreams he had only concentrated on the superficial trimmings.

'I love painting.' he said in attempt to conceal.

'That's good.' she said and she knew that he was lying again. But she was decent. She didn't revel in trampling people, for she understood that it takes all kinds to make a world and she took little pleasure in faulting the poor and weak. She had acquired a bounty of patience and tolerance because of the country in which she was forced to quickly become accustomed. She no longer wished to hold her standards up to the sky. Besides she liked him. They had a few more drinks as the party progressed.

'Let's get out of here and go somewhere else.., this place is getting to me… apart from you there's nothing else here for me' he said.

'Yes let's' she said not realizing that she had said it. She had unwittingly lost control of herself and the evening realizing this, she changed her mind.

'On second thoughts…,' she said, 'I think I'd rather stay here.'

'But it's slow' he retorted, there was a plea in his voice.

'I quite like it.' She said.

'Look we can creep out of here and have the world.' he said sounding a little comical.

'I never said that I wanted anything.' she said.

Romano walked up to them, tapped her on the shoulder and said 'Mustapha.'

She was a little startled, but didn't show it, she was good at concealing her feelings.

'What about Mustapha?' she said

'He asks me to get you, now, he says come now!'

'I feel ill…' she said looking away from the two of them. She didn't like being summoned, especially now that she was making a new friend

Akin stood, nodded to Romano and walked away slowly.

'I want to go.' Binta said turning towards him. 'I'm on my way, you can come with me. I'll tell Mustapha that I'm leaving…'

They both walked away from the seat leaving Romano, alone and suspicious, guarding the empty bench.

III

The pitch-black darkness had passed and a lighted silver-grey sky indicated the emerging dawn. Binta and Akin sat in the car and headed for his room at the hotel. They stripped in the cool room as Stevie Wonder's 'Summer Soft' played on cassette. They made love for the first time as Akin pushed her on her back, spread her legs an entered her warmth, in one elastic and elongated motion. They did it twice, perfectly.

Before this he had been very lonely. Sleeping with her for the first time was different. It was not the simple release of tension that he had previously experienced with his one night stands. His vacant eyes stared into grey space as silver dawn trickled like a creeping ghost into the room, a lightening pale, as he tried to convince himself that nothing special was happening to him. But it gnawed at his spirit, for the chemistry was right. And there was in him a feeling of togetherness.

Binta felt it too. And she knew that day, when she touched his smooth skin in the blue room that she was in love with Akin. She sat up and looked at the diamond ring on her finger. She realized that she was tied to Mustapha, she could see no way out, she was the panic-stricken woman trapped in a house on fire, its flames growing wild ready to engulf her. She was unable to awaken from the burning dream. And her new love further sealed her escape.

NINETEEN

THURSDAY 2ND MAY 1985

In the suite next to Musa Ahmed, four men waited. They could almost hear the second hand of time ticking through their lives. They had attached to the telephone line in his suite a tape recorder which switched on automatically when the phone was in use. A bearded man in a silk dressing gown sat quietly in the lounge of the suite smoking a pipe and reading '*The Man Died', a* book which suited the drudgery of their surveillance task. A younger man sat opposite him smoking Benson and Hedges and playing solitaire on the coffee table. There was one soldier seated beside the door and one who operated the equipment. There was an electronic stethoscope attached to the wall separating Musa Ahmed's suite from theirs; this equipment, a very sensitive microphone fitted with a suction cup allowed them to hear and to record all that took place within Musa Ahmed's suite. Even though the men were outside the suite they were inside it.

On the coffee table there was a bottle of scotch which the younger man swigged liberally as he smoked. The soldier at the door stripped down two pistols and cleaned them. They had been in the suite five days now and there had been little contact with the outside world. Their alcohol intake increased steadily as tension mounted slowly. Even though they were all used to this kind of work it still put their nerves on edge. It was a long wait and the bearded man, his pipe in hand, paced in front of the glass sliding doors that looked across the port channel. 'Make me a coffee' the bearded man ordered the young man, who walked into the kitchen, made the coffee and returned with a full pot and a cup. He poured a cup for the bearded man.

'Thanks' the older man said ingratiated 'have a cup yourself.' he said

'Okay.' said the younger man. He fetched and poured himself a cup

The bearded man put some scotch in his black coffee.

'Try some scotch in your coffee It gives it a good edge.' He said

'Thanks.' he said receiving the bottle of scotch and poured himself a couple of tots.

'Good, isn't it?'

'Yes, it's good'

They both sipped on the laced coffee silently.

'Hell!' complained the bearded man, 'I can't wait to move in on him, I think we have enough, but we instructions from the department are that we must wait until he tries to move in on the ADC... then, we shall be certain of his treasonable plan' he continued, looking tired and frustrated.

'Let's play cards,' the younger man suggested.

'Do you play well?'

'Yes.'

'What will it be?'

'I like rummy.'

'Be warned!' the older man cautioned while closing his book, 'I play well and for money.'

'Will ten Naira be enough for a start?' the younger man asked taking up the challenge.

'Yes ten is fine... will you play up to a hundred? I'll *wack* your money o!

'Hah! So you think.'

 They played rummy all night and the bearded man won. He cleared out his opponent by morning. He had dealt like lightning and always had a flush. The sun had come out and yellow rays streaked through the window. The room warmed slightly and the young man rolled his sleeves up and poured the last of the scotch in his coffee cup.

'You have cleaned me out Sah!' he said throwing down the cards on the floor.

'Okay, here, I'll be soft on you...take twenty back,' he said handing him a note.

'No, no… no! I shall win it back, later I will win it all back!' He said courageously.

'How do you know I will still play... it's my choice to play again' He replied, smiling.

The soldier monitoring the equipment came into the room and they both looked up at him

'I have heard from H.Q…' he reported and handed the bearded man a single sheet of paper. It was very short and in code. He took up his glasses and then took out a small black book from his pocket. He wrote slowly making reference to the book and he was soon finished. He put down his glasses and replaced the book he said

'He meets with the ADC tonight.'

TWENTY

JANUARY 1985

I

She walked into the crowded hotel lobby. Heads turned and looked at her long perfect legs which were exposed by the short grey skirt that hugged her hips. She took no notice of lusty stares that followed her as she moved. It was eight o'clock and a cool fresh ocean breeze came into the open windows of the hotel lobby. She walked into the clean well lit bar and found a quiet grotto from which she could watch all that happened about her. She sat and nervously looked into her hand bag for a cigarette. Her hands trembled as she lit one and smoked it. In the aquarium beside the bar little goldfish floated in their alien surroundings. A waiter walked up to her.

'Welcome Madame, what can I get for you'?'

'Martini, do you have Martini?'

'Yes.'

'You know how I like it-with a little gin and crushed ice,' she said, smoke spewing slowly in artistic gray wisps from her full glossy lips.

'Yes I know how to fix it for you… How is Mustapha?' She nodded,

'He's very well thanks' she said feeling a little pang of guilt in her heart. But she could not help herself. She had not seen Akin since New Year's Day; she had tried to keep away, even now as she sat in the cool bar a small voice in her head whispered to her to keep away. *'Drink up and go home, hold back'* it was saying, the voice of caution and decorum. But at the same time she thought of the last time they had met, made love and held each other. The memories, delicious and sweet made her shudder and she could feel herself weaken, a warm sensation flowed down her body down between her legs as she imagined him. There was soft music from the speakers above the bar and she thought of the past times with Mustapha and the way it had been between them in the beginning. She had thought that she was in love with him, but she had been deceived by the thrill of a first affair and it was only when she had broken out of it that she realized that Mustapha was only a habit, a wonderful first habit. Akin had shown her something new, fresh different, full of emotion and tenderness revealed the past for what it was a lie. Still she felt guilt for she had not been brought up to understand physical pleasure. She felt that in a way she was dirty and all that she was doing was filthy. The truth was she was afraid of her body and the pleasure that it gave her. Mustapha and Akin had set free the carnal animal in her; she was far from the innocence and purity of her background and upbringing. The waiter settled her Martini down before her and she took a large swig and lit another cigarette.

She didn't finish her drinks, stood up, stubbed out her cigarette and left a twenty Naira note under the glass for the waiter. She went to the reception and called him.

'Hello Akin, it's Binta, I'm coming up.' She said.

Her ears popped a little as the lift raced to the eleventh floor; she came out and walked to his room. She was suddenly afraid, should she turn back? She thought, but it was too late. He had already opened the door.

'Binta.' he said embracing her' why didn't you call me like you said?'

'I was sick…er... I travelled home up north.' she said, lying.

'Come in, come in.' He said.

She walked in, slowly, deliberately accentuating the sway of her hips. For a few seconds she could not speak. Akin was a little nervous having been taken by surprise.

'I'd like a drink please, I'm so, so thirsty.' She said

'Sorry, I was just going to offer you one.' He said 'I have some wine, do you like wine?'

'Yes, I'd love some wine, well you know what they say whisky makes you frisky and that wine makes you fine…' she said giggling nervously.

'I will just get some good red wine' he said pretending that he had been born to drinking wine.

She walked to the window and looked out across towards the little shanties of *Maroko*.

Akin took up a corkscrew and struggled with the bottle.

What do you do up here, during the day you have an office?' She asked as she strutted about the suite.

'Oh no baby, I aint got no office, I kinda just stay here and make some business you know, finding customers. I really like the way a hotel can make things easy, no worries about looking for a house.' He replied.

'Ah yes, business, we must all do some sort of business to stay alive. But it must cost though? Wouldn't a house or an apartment be cheaper?'

'No, not to me, I got to really move around and so I prefer a hotel.'

They both sat opposite each other and Akin poured her a drink.

'Fine wine eh?' she said trying to get him to talk.

'Yes' he said staring at her. He sat down, fixated and didn't touch his drink. He realized that he hadn't noticed how elegant her hands were, he hadn't noticed the soft dimples that adorned her cheeks, but it was the eyes, her dark and mysterious eyes that seemed to pull him to her. He realized then that she was a gem, truly exceptional in her beauty. He was no longer nervous, she had calmed him with her look and he sat watching her every move with the curiosity of a child. Suddenly, there was nothing else on his mind but her; he imagined her slender body, her firm breasts, and her pointed nipples, hard and erect.

He was tempted to remember her soft velvety smooth skin and her warm almost electric tongue all over him. Akin did not know when he leaned over to her and kissed her lips. He did not recognize his own voice when he said, 'Binta I must make love to you ...now.' and she stood, as innocent looking as ever and began to undress. He walked up to her and helped her. Binta was no longer in control of herself, naked she took him by the hand and walked him into the bedroom of the suite. There she helped him undress, quickly, eagerly, covering his flesh with little kisses as she exposed it. Her breathing quickened as she pushed him down on the hard bed, lips glued together in a French kiss. Binta was surprised by her own eagerness and her loss of all inhibitions. She had previously been a passive partner relaxed and waiting to be encouraged and satisfied by her man. She was now for the first time taking an active part wanting him to satisfy her and also at the same time wanting to give pleasure to him. Akin was a little overtaken by the turn of events but he eagerly followed her orders as she pulled his head and mouth onto nipples. She guided him into her and rode him to exhaustion, their bodies wet with perspiration as they lay, intertwined in blissful satiety. Akin closed his eyes and Binta kissed him on the cheek and whispered 'Well done darling, well done,' Akin smiled, he could almost hear the scream of 'hooray!' in his head. Binta liked to talk in bed, especially after she had just made love. It was as though her body had been elevated to another plane, her mind was active, alert in a positive way. She talked to Akin, really to herself for she did not wait for a reply as she stared up at the ceiling as she covering both of them up with a warm blanket as the temperature had dropped a little.

'You know I dreamt often of this. I woke often and thought of you beside me' she said almost talking to herself. 'I knew that it would be good, being with you again, but this is far more than I expected great!' she said, almost screaming euphorically. Akin had been overcome by her and he was silent. Binta looked up talking aloud to herself, moving her full lips almost erotically. Akin watched her; he could see the sparkle in her clear eyes that gave away the true joy that was in her heart.

'You know Akin, things have been really down for me and honestly I really haven't ever had anything of my own, not in the way that I have you.' Akin stirred, surprised by the words, not really understanding her meaning.

'...I just don't know Akin,' she continued, sounding a little desperate. 'I really don't know what to think anymore. You see maybe you are what I've needed, what I've hoped for all this time, I might even have conjured you up. Maybe the way I feel about you is all false. Oh I'm so confused - I can no longer discern between fantasy and reality.' She was soon asleep in his arms but as her eyes closed she made a wish. She wished that it would all stay like this forever. She felt a sharp but deliciously sweet pain in her heart; Pleasure.

TWENTY-ONE

JANUARY 1985

I

She was an observant creature and she often went to visit him in his hotel room. She was curious about human nature, and as she could not understand herself, she sought to find clues of herself in other people. She found him odd, and yet every new day brought her to notice some new facet of his personality. Akin was deceptively shallow, even though he was not entirely stupid. Slowly, ever so slowly, like the time from bud to flower, she began to understand him. And he was not so foolish, so empty. She was patient, not only out of curiosity, but because she liked to experience the world, to feel it, and as such she could not hurry nature or people. She was willing to wait. It was only after many weeks that she realized that all he wanted was a chance. For his yearning was clad in a veneer of material desire. She had thought initially that all he wanted was the money, the flash, the panache. She was wrong. Akin belonged to that small group of human achievers who sought more than mere existence. She felt his desire to be a part of the world, to matter, to be more than just a component. He wanted to be noticed in the scheme of things. And without that recognition from the world, he was to his own considerations a walking corpse. Unfortunately, he was not born with a silver spoon and this made it almost impossible for him to be anything but obscure in a country such as theirs. That was the problem. She watched his unspoken frustrations as they tore his insides and subdued his entire being and she learnt a little about herself. She found that she was not alone in the pursuit of happiness and that some were further away from it than she. But she was rich; at least she had time for happiness. She found Akin to be hungry, for he had been born poor, and she felt it. He treated everything as though it were an escaping meal. She found that he talked little but always asked questions, direct and incisive questions, the replies to which he listened attentively as his mind gorged itself with every little bit of information obtained. He fed on her mind in conversation, her body when he made love selfishly, like a confirmed Casanova, using her and spending himself. He saw in her aristocratic demeanor, her dress, her perfect English, the world that he had always desired, for she had been educated in the material things dress, wine, language, literature, art; she had been well finished and as far as her people in the north were concerned, finished off. He overtly mocked her '*Oyinbo*' behavior, but secretly he revered her. She was to him a fantasy. For through her, he would learn to see what he would ordinarily have missed.

She noticed the difference between them. She knew that he was not one of her kind. But she was a little confused, she had not settled well into her country and it was compounded by her late maturity. She noticed also, along with their differences, a certain equality that transcended their social status. She felt it most when he held her and their bodies, their spirits, were intertwined. It was there at the times when he touched her and she touched him.

She would lie awake at times, when they had made love as he would lie sleeping in her arms, and she would stare into space, into nothingness and she would be safe, safe in his warm arms as her world raged about her; Mustapha, the dwindling Mustapha, the deceit that she had taken to in running to Akin, her father, the wild country, the whole rat race would be relegated to a second rate reality as she lay awake in love. And even then she could feel, through her female intuition, the impermanence of it all.

She would feel it, always there in the background, for the more she grew attached to him the worse it became, and it was the bittersweet mix, of the pain and the pleasure. And she remembered what she had told him about their affair. It had been on the second meeting after the party; the intensity of their friendship had subdued and he had asked her what she wanted him to do for her. She understood his question as being, what do you want of me? Yes, the words were still clear in her head for she had been truthful when she said it. 'I don't want the bad parts' she had said, 'not all the jealousy, hate, suspicion and bitterness that loving someone can generate... I want the good bits, the fondness, the joy and all the nice things that come with companionship... life is too short Akin... much too short. There is no excellence, no purity, and no truth. That's why I don't care if you have other women, why should I? I have Mustie. My dearest and darkest Mustie...All that I want from you is you, all of you when we are together... I want it to be that when we are together we are both happy, that there are no tears and that we find comfort in each other... There is no time and I have already had my chance. This is really a small reprieve, I know it, and it is a little something to wet my parched lips, so let us not waste it...' She seemed to have had said it all, an indication that she had grown and had abandoned her rose colored spectacles of youth, as it was between them, a little solace in a tempestuous sea.

TWENTY TWO

It was not Akin's intention to allow his emotions take control of his mind. But he could hardly have been blamed for the way in which this happened with Binta. This is not to say that she was the most beautiful girl he had ever met in his life, she was; almost. But, because, he was always conscious of the fact that he had no control over certain aspects of his life. Fate often played games with the emotions of human beings. Realizing this, Akin accepted his lot in the same way that he accepted the fact that his liaison with Binta was bound to be secret, if either of them wanted to live very long. They both found that the secrecy and the shrouded nature of their friendship made it all the more delicious.

He would often try not to call her and he would go out alone to some bar or the other where he would get sloshed on his own. But that did not often help. He had even tried paying prostitutes to keep him company. But they were much too sleazy for his mood. He found that nothing would quench his thirst for Binta but Binta. He had to have her with him. He would often go back to the hotel and call her in the middle of the night. 'Can you please come over Binta, I need you!' The words had been difficult at first but after the first few times he began to find 'I need you' quite easy to say.

Binta on the other hand, had become altogether less inhibited. She was able to tell him exactly how she felt and said 'I need you' with a natural ease. This was probably because she was a woman and had as such been brought up to need and not be ashamed of her needs. But still she did not tell all. Instead, she took to writing in a journal little bits as her feelings often overcame her. Her small secret book contained the things she had felt and done that she was unable to tell anyone. She found that after she met Akin her entries became more elaborate. If Akin had a chance to stumble across and peep into her book, he would have read: '*January 1985- Everything seems to have happened to me last night. This year, I hope to God that it is my year, entered with a bang. I met a man or boy as I'm not sure which and I think something magnificent will happen. I'm sure of it. I can't even remember what he said or what I said but I remember being in his arms. But I am afraid, and sad. What will happen to me? What will happen to us? What will happen to all three of us; Mustapha, Akin and me. I feel that I shouldn't call him. Yes I'll leave it as it is, 1985 you sly fox you've really got me in a fix now...*'

Most of what she wrote was often confused as she wrote quickly, never reading it over. But somewhere in the rambling sentences in her little diary there was to be found much wisdom. Some of the things she wrote were surprisingly apt and real. She once wrote: '*I am no longer ashamed of my person and my human form. If I like sex, it is not something that I should be ashamed of. I have come to terms with being a woman and at my age the greatest gift I have to give is my heart and of course my body. It would be a shame if I could not use my body well. What then would I have it for? I no longer feel shy about Akin, I can do anything physically possible to him and with him like today we...*'

Sometimes though, she found that she was not always so nice to him. She found that the people closest to her were on the receiving end of her sharp, sometimes acidic, tongue. It was because she was so much in love with him that she was sometimes mean to him. Usually at the end of the day she would go home, having treated him thoroughly badly, and cry herself to sleep. She wrote on one of her tearful evenings exactly how she felt about it all. '*I am such a fool sometimes, because I do the wrong things and then expect them to be right. I do not listen to the oldest rules in the book . . . . Never love someone that you can't have. That love will break your heart and the pain and the pleasure which love brings will haunt you, its daggers pierced deep into your heart.*'

TWENTY-THREE

MARCH 1985

Torrential tropical rain; There came with it a wind that bent the trees and blew off their leaves. In his study Mustapha looked out into the day at waterlogged garden and the blossoming flame tree, its red flowers floating in the swimming pool. He was angry, for he had been betrayed.

On his desk lay an envelope full of blown up black and white photographs of a man and a woman. She was a most beautiful woman with a handsome man. They were seen at dinner, going into a hotel, leaving it, driving a car. They had been watched carefully for also in the envelope there was a report. In it, the photographed events were recorded, dated and timed. Now Mustapha knew everything. He knew how many nights they had spent together. And it hurt him. He set his mind on ways of getting even. Even as he planned, he knew that whatever action he would take would hurt him, heart of stone or not, he had felt a lot for her but he could not think of forgiveness. He was without the understanding of mercy and could neither accept it nor bestow it.

He thought of his life and he almost bent double with pain. The feelings emerged unexpectedly, those bouts of emotional agony that can escape even from a heart of stone. He had taken much pain in his time but nothing was worse than being orphaned and he still remembered how it had come, this loneliness of his. How he had achieved his dreams, he saw the full picture of his life in comparison to those of others, and often he slipped into reminiscences of the past. A cigarette, a drink, beneath the yellow lamplight on his desk he scrutinized the pictures. There was jealousy and envy which propelled him and he vowed to solve his problem the only way he knew how. But he would have to be careful. A close farewell is never easy.

Slanting rain, silver droplets cascading through air, deep rumbles of thunder, flashes of electric lightning, and the storm raged outside blowing nature about as he contemplated murder.

TWENTY-FOUR

THURSDAY 2ND MAY 1985

Their conversation was drowned in music. Musa and the smiling handsome young man sat unnoticed in the dark corner of the elegant nightclub in Ikeja. Musa watched, as he had several beers. Musa drank champagne. They talked about everything except the subject that was on the tip of their tongues. Nnamdi was also a wily fox. They watched the female vocalist in her thirties performing. Apart from the black faces they might have been in Europe. This was the rich man's club.

'Come over here,' Nnamdi beckoned waving at two women sitting close by.

'Let me take the tall one, you can have the small pretty one' he whispered to Musa poking him in the ribs and slapping him on the back. Evidently he didn't know Musa too well. Damn it, thought Musa, their private conversation would be invaded. He had been watching his wet lips as he drank, sounding him out, he wanted to know in which camp he would fall. Nnamdi was ADC to a key senior officer. He was known for his efficiency. There were advantages in having him on his side. Musa had to take care of all the details which included the plans, the timing, the temperament of his colleagues and the government they would form after the takeover and he had to make sure that he was not squeezed out of the plot in the course or its execution as this sometimes happened.

'I don't really like them,' he said holding his glass in the air.

'Come on my friend, I have heard of you... Musa Ahmed...I'm sure you have something waiting for you at home... Na wa oh...' the girls sat down gracelessly. They were overdressed, over perfumed, overfed and masked in hideous war paint like make-up that confirmed to all that they were prostitutes.

'What do you take?' Nnamdi asked.

'Chamm- Penn!' the tall one said as the little one nodded in agreement. In no time they were all drinking fizz.

Musa fingered the crystal glass in feminine fashion as he mused, his mind like the multicolored disco lights that Flashed around him, touching varied topics. His face was a veneer of placid civility; he was a very difficult man to know and understand. His beauty like that of Adonis himself, flawless and pure, never failed to attract people to him. They knew him from the outside and no more, many had suspected he was a homosexual but none had proof. There was hardly much proof of anything to do with him.

His past was less interesting. He was the fourteenth child of an inconsequential cattle owner from Gembu in the Mambilla Plateau. His record at a hardly known village school was colorless. He was one of the lucky few nothings that sometimes slipped through the system. Luck had nothing to do with his progress though. Musa had schemed his way through school, passed his exams by blackmailing the smartest boy in the class and threatening his teachers with all sorts of things. It was easier in the army, for so many had a skeleton in the cupboard. Musa was, from his past record, cut out for intelligence work. In spite of his past lack of academic brilliance he had vision. He had in his dreams of the future seen more to life than cutting one's nails and driving cattle in the Savannah. Now as he sat drenched in alcohol he could visualize the ultimate in his desires. He could see it all as if it was by divine right laid at his feet. He was not a Christian, but as he sipped the cold wine he remembered a line from a prayer he had heard so often murmured by Christians.

'*For Thine is the kingdom, the power and the glory forever and ever...*' That was it, he thought. Power! Nnamdi and the two girls talked briskly, Musa didn't listen. The small fat girl put her fingers between her melon-like breasts, brought out a slim gold lighter and with it lit herself a cigarette. The music, imbued with an excess of bass, banged in Musa's head in a dissonant crescendo. He was not moved to dance as an agonizing ache that had been nurtured in his head exploded. He stood up, swayed a little, said his quick goodbyes and left. Nnamdi, euphoric at the sight of impending satiety, smiled, got up and led Musa out by the arm.

Musa touched his arm lightly, as they walked through the hall towards the entrance. If the girls hadn't come he would have had a better chance of sounding him out. He had almost got his fix on Nnamdi. But now he wasn't too sure.

He had every reason to believe that Nnamdi would go along with him. Ostensibly, he liked money, girls and the good life. That was a clear enough indication that he would also desire power. For power is the father of all pleasures. But there were still exceptions to every rule, would he and could he take the chance? Nnamdi was well informed. He was great at drinking; he too could extract information from the most faithful of friends. Musa suspected that he had got wind of the plot. It may not have come from a reliable source or from any source at all. It may have been a feeling, a gut feeling, like those of great warriors who feel victory before the fight. The doorman opened the back door for them and they walked out. Musa realized that he was running out of time and distance. He could not approach this man again as it would look very suspicious. This was his only chance. The adrenalin pumped through him as he prepared to make his move, say his piece. It was like that with power, it was worth a couple of risks. He wet his lips, parted them and spoke.

'I came today to tell you about the future...'Musa said 'I know!' Nnamdi said, cutting him short, '...what you called me here for, it is possible, very dangerous, but possible that I can help you.' With that he knew that he had won him over.

TWENTY-FIVE

MIDNIGHT THURSDAY 2ND MAY 1985

He was slightly tired, having had too much wine at the night club, it had been worth it though, sometimes it was necessary to loosen a man's tongue with alcohol. He walked out of the elevator on the eleventh floor and turned left towards his suite. He had to be up at five in the morning for the airport.

The final meeting was scheduled to take place in Geneva at a small unobtrusive hotel. They would rendezvous there, after the official meeting with prospective defense contractors. It was perfect cover. He turned the key to the door and entered. It was dark. He imagined that he could smell pipe tobacco. It must be from the next suite he thought. He switched the lights on and stared at the three AK47 assault rifles pointed at him. There were four men in the room, three of them uniformed soldiers and seated comfortably in a chair was a bearded intelligence officer in mufti.

'Don't move sah!' one of the soldiers said. 'Empty your pockets slowly and drop the pistol on the floor, kick it to me…and crawl here face down!' the man in mufti ordered.

'Good Musa... That's very good.' He said and he picked up his pipe and lit it, puffed the sweet tobacco and smiled.

'You failed sir' he continued. 'You should be more careful, how you could have forgotten that an officer of your rank could escape surveillance? We have had our finger on you for the past year. Normally we did not mind you making a little cash, it's allowed. We all have to retire.'

Musa Still shocked, stood fixed, speechless as though he had seen a ghost.

'Come on sit down, we have been here for hours, you make this work too difficult for us.... I am tired of your champagne; you have more than ten thousand Naira worth of it here, while some people can't even buy fanta or eat a meal. '

Musa, the quarry, showed no signs of losing his cool.

'Come on get to it! I hope you have clearance this, class 'A' clearance?' he said feigning confidence.

'Come on shut up shut up your dirty mouth, you saboteur treason is no small game!' the man said and slapped him hard across the face; the three soldiers stepped closer and pointed their guns in his face. The man laughed, a shrill triumphant cackle filled the room.

'Musa Ahmed Sah!' He said cynically 'we are not here to take orders from you... Major or no major... what the hell, I could kill you now but those are not my orders... give us all your money first.' He demanded.

'Musa stood up; the three soldiers followed him closely as he walked to the closet in which he kept his clothes. He looked over his shoulder at the man in the chair, the lamp behind his head lit like a halo. He remembered his face, yes he thought that's that fool from Section B.25. When I get into power he'll disappear, he said to himself. He still had the burning ambition and the steely vengeance of a soldier in him. He took out a brown crocodile leather attaché case, opened it and brought it back and gave it to them. It was full bundles of hundred dollar bills and large denomination Naira notes.

'Thank you, you are kind. But that is not going to get you off the hook.'

Musa's heart sank; he finally realized the depth of trouble in which he was. It was all clear now, one of his contacts had done him in, and one of his prospective co-plotters had spilt the beans and guaranteed the safety of his own skin and probably also some substantial monetary reward. It was something that as a Security Officer he had done in the past, he had uncovered at least three coup plots. It was different and distressing to be at the receiving end of the stick.

'We have been well informed of your plan Musa...' the bearded man said.

'If not for this money we were instructed to beat the life out of you, as you will agree these British army boots are probably the best at damaging dentition?' he continued pointing at the boots of one of the uniformed soldiers...

'But as an officer and a generous one at that I shall pass over the opportunity.' He continued.

'Now ... what you must do is this...'

They sat talking till five a.m. and he dressed for the airport, one of the intelligence officers was to go with him to Geneva. He was almost broken, to save his life he would have to hand over his accomplices to the Security Services and for certain they would be shot. Also, he would forfeit the money to be used for operational arrangements, and would, most difficult of all, arrange to have Mustapha killed. Even after all of this was done he remained at their mercy. In African politics, mercy was a diamond, rare and expensive. They left for the airport.

TWENTY- SIX

SATURDAY 11 MAY 1985

'So Inspector Muna-Muna, what do you want me to do?' Binta asked as she stared at Muna-Muna's face in the sun. They walked down Bar Beach.

'So?'

'Then you must find out whether that man wey you tell me for your letter, whether him know people for airport wey bin help am.' She had already told him a little about Mustapha, it had been difficult as she was not used to betrayal.

'Yes there is one chap, a customs officer, I saw him once in Mustapha's house, and I think he could be involved.' She replied.

'Then you know wetin you go do eh, you go see whether you fit find am, tell am say I want see am for one beer parlor, I go describe am to you.' Muna-Muna went on to tell her how she would describe Madame Calabar's beer parlor to the Officer.

It was a warm afternoon, the sea breeze passed over them and on to the Island. Waves broke on the white sand, white surf bubbled on the eroding beach. They walked on past the palm-covered sun shades, past white crosses of ocean-inspired prayer houses. She smiled to herself at having been able to predict Muna-Muna. She had known that she would tell him of Akintola Noga at least she would not tell him all about Mustie directly. Akintola Noga could do that; he could be Judas to him. But she could not help wondering if she was doing the right thing. She knew of Mustapha and his killing streak, she may have been sending him to his death. She should have worried about herself for she was already entangled in the spider's web.

They walked on and she took off her shoes and waded barefoot in the surf. He watched her as though she were mad. 'It's good for you, very refreshing' she said. He ignored her and stopped to buy some cigarettes and sweets from a *Mallam* in the shade of the beach huts.

'You want chewin-gorm?'He asked offering her some bubble gum.

'No, thanks Muna, it's bad for your teeth.' she said.

She looked out to the distant horizon and then up at the blue sky and she remembered her dreams, her and Akin's dreams that floated in her blue memory like the white cumulus clouds she saw across the blue sky above her.

'Muna... How do you know he'll come?' she asked.

'Tell am say him must come!' Muna-Muna said with authoritative emphasis.

'That's hardly enough.' Binta replied.

'Okay tell am say me I get information wey I go take report am, say him don dey chop bribe from that other man, wetin be him name?...Mustapha...Mustapha, tell am say I get information say Mustapha dey bribe am well well.'

'Will he believe me?'

'Ah... ah, no worry about believe, when him hear say I talk say I go report am, fear go catch am and him body go begin shake... abi you think say him go like go prison?.., Him no go mind say na true we talk, him go come make him make sure say no be true... you hears tell am say...say...I get hot informations! Very... hot, hot informations!' He declared.

'Okay I'll give it a try.' She said.

They came to a beer selling kiosk and Muna-Muna could not resist the temptation of his life juice.

'Make we take one beer now?' he suggested.

'Inspector Muna... what do you take me for? Do you think I'd drink in a lowly and tacky place like that?' she said.

'Na you *sabi*, if you no want beer take minerals, I sure say Coca Cola go dey.' He said licking his lips

'I wouldn't be caught dead drinking in a seedy little place like that... one must have some standards you know!' She said flatly.

'Well na you *sabi*, as for me I dey go take one cold beer wash my brain make I begin to plan as I go challenge dis Mustapha' He said walking purposefully towards the little wooden hut.

'Well suit yourself, I'm off, bye.' She slipped on her shoes and walked back towards her car, started up and drove off. Muna-Muna watched her go, wiped his face with a handkerchief and proceeded into the kiosk.

'Old boy,' he said to the little boy selling drinks '*knack* me one cold beer now, now!' He instructed after which he smiled awaiting his favorite brew.

TWENTY-SEVEN

SATURDAY 11TH MAY 1985

I

Dusk; Two men sat beneath the faded *'Guinness is good for you'* poster at Madame Calabar's. Akintola Noga sat on the wooden bench beneath the green bulb that lit the front verandah of the bar. Opposite him was Muna-Muna. They both smoked cigarettes as the evening traffic passed by raising dust on them.

'Na wetin you go take?' Muna asked as the drinks were on him, 'as for me na biar I de take, na him betta pass.'

'*Mesef* I go take. Beer,' Akintola Noga replied.

'Our Madame O; Bring us two Star beers, quick quick!' Muna-Muna commanded.

It was their first meeting and Muna-Muna looked at the fresh-faced plump man carefully, examining every expression, facial contortion, mannerism and even unintended action for innuendoes. He was looking at his heart and not the mask that men so often hold before the mirror. He looked at his gold-adorned fingers and from this he could tell that he was a man of material things. He knew of the enjoyable empty things that often satisfy men. Akintola Noga too tried to size him up. On the first meeting they both played the same game.

'You know say I bin get pickin… I mean my sister pickin who be your namesake.' Muna said.

'I no been know, it's good' Noga replied.

'Which kind of life we dey live *sef?*'Noga asked, feigning sadness.

'Yes I bin like that boy too much.' Muna said.

Noga watched through his brown eyes the sad, dejected expression on Muna-Muna's unshaven face. He wondered what it would be like at that age. He was twenty-seven but, his over-weight build made him look older, like a man in his Forties, roly and spreading. From his relative youth he could see for himself a more rosy future, a quick easy climb to the good life. He certainly did not consider the possibilities of retirement and penury.

'You were a force man?' he said exposing his thoughts.

'Yes na police force I bin dey,' Muna-Muna said.

'Police... that one na strong place oh my friend.' Noga relaxed a little, his thoughts still essentially comparing futures, he had no cause to worry he told himself. After all, there's a big difference between Police and Customs. Customs was where it was all at. The beers came, cold and sweating green bottles and Madame Calabar set the bottles down in front of them and leaned across Muna, her musky smell filling his nostrils as she opened the beer.

'Una want chop pepper soup or snail... I get *eba* and a*fang* soup too?' she asked.

'Me I want chop snail. I too dey like to chop de *congomeat*.' Muna replied as he expertly filled His glass with cold beer.

'What of you *Oga*, you go chop snail too?' she asked looking at Noga.

'De pepper soup e dey sweet?' Akintola Noga asked.

'Ah my pepper soup de sweet too much... *chei!* Ee go sweet you finish your head go scatter!' she said waving her index finger in mock warning and flashing her white teeth in a tradesman's smile.

'Okay now, make you bring this your pepper soup wey dey sweet.' Noga said smiling and buying the offer.

She went off to fetch their delicacies and they both resumed their, thoughts and words lubricated by lager.

'How do you know Binta Yar Mouktar?' Noga asked him.

'You know say we Policemen too know people... she be my sister *pickin*, the one wey don die, him friend' Muna said trying to explain. 'You sure say you no bin know that my *pickin* Akin?'

Noga remembered Akin pretty well; he had been a part of the plot for his arrest. He was actually the one who had even handed over the briefcase full of drugs to him at the airport but something, his sixth sense, told him that that was better kept a secret. He could feel, as most cowards do, the strength of Muna-Muna's convictions. He sensed the aura of power that almost hummed like an energy field around him.

I didn't know that Binta knew Akin; I had only suspected.' He said lying

Muna-Muna stared him squarely, his incisive gaze cutting his spirit. He wasn't sure he liked Noga but somehow it didn't matter much, little really mattered anymore. He had gone through his life clinging on to honesty and honor but now that he was waning, approaching the evening of his life, it all seemed empty, pointless. Ordinarily he should have gone to the Police, but that was a joke; having been a Policeman, he realized that it would solve absolutely nothing; it may even have gotten him killed. He slurped his beer and wondered how best to deal with this man. He wouldn't tell him about the tape. He would use blackmail as a last resort, only a last resort. He still had some good in him.

The snails and the pepper soup came and they suspended again their feeble conversation, Akin's incident and all that surrounded it had slowly become an obsession to him; Muna-Muna lived for nothing else. That youthful fire and zest that often comes in a man's twenties had come to him in his late fifties. He had begun to see not the trees but the wood. He understood his objective; to vindicate murder and he did not care how he would succeed in doing it. He hardly cared who would be trampled in his attempt to achieve this. He was spurred on by the thirst for victory, engulfed by revenge. He too, in the most concealed and curious way, had come under the spell of the most potent of all drugs, power.

II

They had several Star beers and Muna-Muna paid the bill. Neither of them was drunk, they were both pretty good at drinking and it would take more than a few casual beers to have any significant effect on them, and they walked off to a night spot down the road.

'You never go Coconut Inn before?' Muna-Muna asked Noga.

'No I never go' Noga said.

'Ah... ah! Na there, the betta *tittees* dey... make I dash you Angelina I sure say you go like am, she too sabi how to bend waist' Muna-Muna said smiling broadly, fiendishly.

'She go suck your blood so tey... you go quench!' he continued, laughing out loud and slapping Noga's back. They stumbled across a deep fetid concrete gutter in front of a pea green, gloss painted bungalow with multi-colored fairy lights, most of the bulbs dead, around the front porch. There was a stunted, dry and hardly fruiting coconut palm that stood limply, in part existence, in front building.

'You see the coconut? You see am!' Muna-Muna said

'Yes' Noga replied.

'Das why this na de Coconut Inn!' he said smiling foolishly and murdering a poor joke. They went in through a corridor and music, sweet highlife melodies, came from the courtyard beyond. Noga stopped at a bar, a makeshift affair with an un-shaded naked yellow glaring bulb, and asked the muscle-bound boy behind the chicken wire grill to give him a couple of beers. Just under the bar he read written on a black board in colored chalk:

" XXX *Performing T- Nite* XXX *Commander Victor Pedro and his Congo Revolutions, sweet Congo highlife beat* XXX *come one, come all* XXX *only N1 Flat* xxx *till day break.* XXX"

The boy in the cage took the beer money and asked aggressively;

'What of the money you go pay for the dance now?!' Noga handed him the extra. As they walked in, a fat gaudy prostitute came up to Noga and slipped her arms into his; 'Daahling na you be my customer?' she said squeezing him.

'Come on will you get away!' Muna-Muna barked and she quickly left Noga alone.

'Na your husband?' she asked contemptuously hissing, and returning to the dark eaves.

'That one no be Angelina, when you see am, na you wey go take your hand find am' Muna-Muna said smiling. They walked into a small yard at the back, full of people, twisting and dancing in highlife euphoria. Commander Pedro sweated on a small wooden stage, cigarette in hand, he crooned in French and broken English as the Revolutions blasted melodious trumpet into the air. They sat at a small, rusting and wobbling metal table and on dusty chairs. There were many free girls that hovered, in an attempt to mix, around the dance area. Muna waved at a woman and beckoned her.

'Angelina, Angie comes, come!' he shouted and she walked towards their table, slowly and erotically swaying her generous hips, her cigarette smoking between her lips.

'Angie: My sister... how you dey?' Muna greeted as he grabbed her waist. She was quite plump and fair with tellingly bleached skin and her teeth were brown and nicotine-stained.

'Who be dis?' she asked giving Noga a quick glance.

'Na my friend wey de work for customs.' He replied

At the word 'customs' she smiled and moved her chair close to Noga.

'Him fine O.' She cooed, not shifting her gaze. Noga swigged, slightly shaken and spoke;

'You want drink?' he asked.

'Yes, big stout. 'She said

He got up. 'You too...another drink?' he asked Muna-Muna as he walked away. Muna-Muna whispered to the woman in Noga's absence. They both laughed. Pedro, Commander of highlife swayed rhythmically on stage, his white clothes drenched in perspiration and the beat rocked the yard, melodious trumpet blast mixed with rhythmical dance inspiring bass guitar, shoes sliding on sand and concrete, twisting jerking bodies as the men and women danced a rhythmical pelvic shuffle. The Coconut Inn jumped as Noga returned with the bar boy in trail, drinks in hand.

'This... one... na de Angelina O!' Muna said.

She held Akintola Noga's hand and pulled him towards her.

'Make we dance!' she said almost ordering him and they stood, found a niche on the crowded floor and began to twist and jerk rhythmically.

III

An hour later, Akintola Noga found himself in a pale blue room; he lay naked, still drunk and satiated with the bleached body in varying cocoa shades beside him.

'Take hot drink now?' she said as she pushed a half bottle of abrasive brandy to him, he swigged, the cheap rough drink, coarse spirit burnt his throat, warmed his chest and woke him up. It somehow straightened him and he sat up and groped for his clothes. He began to dress and Angelina held his hands away from his shirt.

'Make you stay reach morning now?' she said in a thick sleazy voice. He dressed faster. He hurried out of the room into a corridor that spilled into the yard where the Commander and Revolutions still played, no longer melodious to him; he fell irritated by the scene. He searched for Muna-Muna, who was nowhere to be found, and he was not prepared to search all the rooms for him, besides, he had the funny feeling that he would see him very soon. He left the pea-green thumping Palace and found a taxi He went home to his anti-biotic prophylactics. He was unable to pay the taxi and had to borrow from his house staff as his wallet had been stolen.

TWENTY EIGHT

3RD MARCH 1985

It was morning and dark grey clouds obscured the sun and hid the blue sky. The air was heavy and a quick breeze blew over the lawn rolling dry brown leaves on it. Romano and Akin sat on the garden chairs beside the pool on which the air made several small waves and they ate their breakfast quickly 'It will rain' Romano said in his deep almost guttural voice.

'It will rain very heavy' he repeated.

'Yep, that's why I wanna eat fast rains like bad news man,' Akin said is mouth half full as he strained his newly acquired fake American accent. He had seen many changes in his life and he was no longer a scavenger. His dress; the finely cut navy blue suit, bright spotted bow tie and expensive dark sunglasses to hide his puffy eyes, were an indication of his new status. He was still slim though, in spite of his gluttony he had scarcely put on weight. He had become Romano and Mustapha's right hand man. He was the most effective courier to Europe and he was their main informant on the activities of their pusher in England. He was trusted as much as any could be in such a volatile business.

'You need to be slower' Romano said, pointing at Akin's plate.

'I don wanna eat slow man, life's too fast, too fast to waste it all in eating, I wanna live like speed ,man…y' know really live.'

'My own needs are simple.' Romano said, his simple sounding like '*seem-pool*' 'I don't have any needs man…what I got is an urge....'

Romano said 'let us not waste our tongues…, I have something for you to do, it is very important, it will be very much like your usual operations…'

'Wacha want me to do!' Akin blurted out.

'Patience …'Romano said firmly '…I shall explain it all to you, it is not too difficult, but very important, it will be much unlike your usual operations. It will even be much easier' He went on to explain the task.

Usually Akin would travel first class as a courier to London with the cocaine concealed in a book. Sometimes it was a single large book, sometimes several small ones. The pages were stuck together and hollowed out and bound till they dried, leaving a small space like a safe. It was here that the cocaine and coffee were put in; the coffee was there to conceal the smell. Akin had to run his own risk and a risk which was minimal for he always had enough cash in various currencies to pay his way out of trouble. In comparison to other couriers working for Mustapha he carried much less on him; he travelled with them so that at the destination he would collect the successfully trafficked commodities, pool them together and hand it to their man. For that he was paid 30,000 dollars. Romano explained to Akin that the Mustapha Organization needed certain large sums of money abroad and had to increase their shipment this once. He told him that a briefcase would be given to him after the customs check and that all he would have to do would be to make certain that in London when all the other passengers left the aircraft, he would leave it under his seat and walk out empty handed. For that, he would be paid twice his usual fee. It was dead easy; or so Akin thought.

Thunder bellowed in the bowels of the sky shaking the very centre of the earth. Dark black clouds laden with rain prepared to wash the air, the land, the wind rushed faster blowing the brocade table cloth about and knocking over the Arabian brass coffee pot.

'I can do it' Akin said, 'sure as hell I can do it!' He laughed. The droplets of rain fell, through the atmosphere as they both ran for cover the under the gazebo.

'See just like I said, it rain very heavy' Romano said and he wiped the water from his face with the palm of his hand.

'It rain very heavy.'

TWENTY-NINE

26TH APRIL 1985

He had hardly recovered from his malaria attack, but already he had started working. He couldn't bear to be idle, he was always planning his next move, looking over his shoulder, and it had become a way of life. Orange evening sunlight slanted through large stained-glass windows, bathed in amber light, Mustapha sat. A slim man in a white French suit he wheeled his swivel-chair round to the big glass doors that overlooked the pool. Binta splashed white water as she swam. He looked at her, Junoesque and lithe as she cut through with smooth strokes. His mind went back to Musa Ahmed. As usual he considered several times every major move he made, especially those that were likely to jeopardize his future. He imagined Musa, propelled into the arena of dictatorship, would please benefactors for a little while and then he would turn against them. As the intoxicating and immortalizing fumes of power would make him vain and make him think that he was too important to take orders from anyone. He would then proceed to destroy Mustapha and any others who were reminders of the mortality he sought to forget, 'where would that leave me'? Mustapha asked himself. He realized that he had to do something; he must avoid the wrath of the possible future leader.

Outside, Binta emerged from the pool and Mustapha looked at her. He looked at her face and noticed that she lost the, youthful zestful expression that had warmed her to him. She, like the decadent world to which she had taken, had visibly aged. Mustapha in his search for a solution to his problem decided on insurance. He always protected himself when confronted with the possibility of betrayal. Mustapha walked out of his office through the sliding doors to meet her. The dusk came, with it a cool breeze, spreading bugs and mosquitoes through the tropical stickiness of the island. He decided to make contact.

II

Two days later they picked a man up in the evening standing beside his white Volkswagen Beetle car which was parked near the creek. They drove alongside the creek and could see Ikoyi from Eleke Crescent. Mustapha asked his chauffeur to drive around slowly. In air conditioned comfort they sat and whispered. The bearded passenger held his pipe in his hands, gently stuffing the bowl with tobacco. As they whispered, Mustapha gently coaxing him and promising him heaven; he smoked, filling the darkened interior of the Mercedes sweet grey smoke.

With the evening there came rain, and the drizzle sprayed the windows of the car with silver droplets of water. Mustapha looked out, darkness had come and he could hardly see the man's Volkswagen beetle when they came to it. They stopped and as he got out Mustapha held the arm of his jacket. 'I'm sure I can rely on you,' he said smiling a little and nodding his head, he patted him. Mustapha's usually placid grey eyes twinkled, an evil glint, as they always did when he prepared to do battle.

THIRTY

TUESDAY, 5TH MARCH 1985

Akin awoke, poorly rested and groggy, he stumbled out of bed, almost falling, and groped in the dark; he found the light switch and bathed the room in yellow electric light. It was 5.00am and he had to be at the airport in an hour. He noticed, beside the door, a brown unmarked envelope, that, since it had not been there when he slept, he concluded it had been pushed under the door during the night. He picked it up examined it wearily, it was light and not at all bulky he considered that it was safe enough and opened it. He removed the white paper and he read the unidentifiable script. It read: '*be warned don't go anywhere today, stay in don't go out.*' It was not signed or dated. He examined the envelope and the note again. He was alert now, his mind sharpened by the mystery, as he tore it into small pieces. Binta, he thought, when will she ever grow up?

He had come, over the short time he had knew her, to be very fond of her. She had brought out a gentle trait that he had never imagined existed in him. It was an animal and lustful interest initially. When he first set eyes on her it was a thing of conquest at the time, fuelled by alcohol and drugs he had gone for her, not minding at all that she was Mustapha's. He showered and dressed quickly, he thought of her. Of all of her, physically, spiritually and he for once, thought of the future. He had never really thought seriously of the future, he lived for the present. He usually travelled with only a briefcase, but this time, he went without one as Romano had told him that one would be handed to him in the customs hall. He took his passport, ticket and money and walked down to a waiting taxi in front of the hotel. The fast life had lost all its glitter, as do many things in life, and he was no longer depthless. Maybe it was Binta. It had to have something to do with her. The taxi driver sped down the expressway to the airport and the cool morning air rushed through the Peugeot as they meandered through the thickening morning traffic.

Akin had changed; he had become less thirsty for the wealth, as the intangible feeling that she had bestowed upon him slowly quenched the fire of his thirst. He was maturing like all youth. In his thoughts of the future, he wanted to make a break from Mustapha and Romano and all the fast freewheeling. This brief one would be the final exchange. He would tell Binta of the plan to escape; they would go far away to a faceless life in an unnamed land where they could marinate in their emotions. The whole plan was a dream, like a poorly lit low budget film.

He quickly returned his mind to the matter at hand .He took a tranquilizer to calm his nerves, he was afraid. He would have to make sure of his present assignment. Dreaming often makes time pass and he realized this as they were already at the airport. He paid the taxi driver, leaving him a generous tip. He stepped into the departure hall and walked to the check-in counter slightly subdued, almost floating as a result of the valium.

II

He cut a suave figure as he walked across the departure hall. He looked tall, young looking, vibrant and full of life. His dark grey impeccably tailored suit was befitting of a gentleman. He walked, hands in pockets, to the first class check in counter. There were hardly any other passengers and the man behind the counter looked a little puzzled when he had told him that he had no luggage whatsoever. He stopped at the restaurant and had an instant coffee.

He thought of her again, as the steaming warm fluid flowed into him, warming him. She had not even known of his present journey, he was certain that it would be a piece of cake, and as they had asked him not to tell anyone about his trip, he had told her a lie that he was going up North for a few days to visit his uncle who was a policeman. He didn't want to worry her, for she had recently taken to worrying about him. He lit a cigarette and filled himself with caffeine and nicotine as he waited for the flight to be announced, it was important that there were many in the customs hall when he took the briefcase that was part of the plan.

THIRTY-ONE

THURSDAY, 16TH MAY1985

I

It was a warm still evening; Muna-Muna sat in the sticky humidity of Madame Calabar's eating house. He was alone, lost in his thoughts and his beer. He was a moody man and sometimes melancholy got the better of him. But that too would pass; he wasn't manic depressive, he was quiet. At the worst, his only self destructive action was simply a few bottles of cold beer. For him life's problems could be solved by a good dose of the brew, or so Muna thought. As he sat greedily pouring the frothy liquid down his throat, activity continued about him; the small radio in the corner played melodious highlife by Nico Mbarga and his band, and in the center the room two men crouched over a draughts board and periodically, screamed at one another 'chei I don chop you!' another figure crunched on the bones from his bowl of goat meat pepper soup while outside a Jehovah's Witness preacher translated the Bible into simplistic terms; 'If you no take time…' he said 'Na so Satan go carry your hand put for soup wey dey hot well-well!...', and outside there was from the road a small voice of the little boy who carried a tray on his head, 'sweet buredi, sweet bread!', he cried as he trudged along with his wares. But Muna-Muna was oblivious to the buzzing activity about him, he was numbed by his thoughts and he sat, like an old man reveling in rumination of the past, in a ghost-like trance.

After the experience with Angelina the other night Akintola Noga was not keen to meet with Muna-Muna again. But he had agreed to meet him at Madam Calabar's especially since Binta had told him of the 'hot information!' Somehow he found the old policeman interesting, like all queer fish, intriguing. He walked into the room and looked round, seeing Muna in the corner, he walked up to him.

'Ah… Noga na you?' Muna said looking up.

'How you dey?' Noga replied.

'I dey as I dey' Muna said.

Noga sat down, the seat a little small for him.

'Ole boy, how you come take run that night?' Muna said enquiring about the night at the coconut Inn.

'Me? I been dey look for you, na him I no come see you so I just fade from that sad joint.' Noga replied.

'How Angelina now...? I sure say she been show you pepper!' Muna said smiling broadly. He had unwittingly hit nail on the Head, but Noga preferred to keep quiet about his wallet. He didn't want to look like a fool.

'Na wetin you go booze?' Muna asked.

'No my belle dey worry me, I no want booze today,' Noga replied

'*Haba*...' Muna said. 'Na wetin..? If man no drink then na wetin remain... wetin him go do... a beg take one beer wash your belle.' Muna continued,

'No, no,' Noga said. Muna-Muna ignored his objection.

'Madame!' he said, 'madam 0! ...bring one cold Star for my paddy man here... bring am quick, quick.' He instructed.

Noga was unable to resist the pressure of the drinking man.

They both drank the beer when it came and Noga felt that this was history repeating itself. He had tried to be a little cold to Muna-Muna, but it was not easy, not with his smiling face, seemingly oblivious to the difficulties of life. It was difficult not to be carried along with his odd charisma. Soon, Noga was relaxed and boozing away.

'Make we take another one now, na me go pay for am' Noga said.

'You self...' Muna accused 'you too dey pretends like say you no like beer!' 'Okay, Okay... I like am small.' Noga said.

'Eh, heh, I been see am for your face, you are a beer man' Muna-Muna said as he reached over and tapped him amiably on the shoulder.

Noga laughed falling prey to Muna Muna's friendly overtures. He was happy for he felt he had made a friend, a rare gem in life, and he hoped to get to know Muna better.

'Make we go Coconut Inn?' I hear say Commander Pedro day play there again tonight… Angelina go still dey o!' Muna-Muna suggested mischievously.

'No me I no want go, you know se I get for work tomorrow' Noga replied.

Muna did not push it, it was an insincere offer, he really wanted to pin Noga down and tell him of the plan. But he was also a patient man. He was prepared to wait a while, stalk his prey and get him a little sloshed. It was always an effective method of loosening a man's tongue and besides he also enjoyed the tongue loosening process himself.

II

A short while later, Muna-Muna decided it was time to trap Noga. He had assessed him and had come to the conclusion that it was the only way. They had had four bottles of beer each; Noga was adequately soaked in the intoxicating nectar.

'Eh heh, Noga, I bin want tell you sometin.' Muna said carefully and deliberately, he kept an emotionless face.

'Tell me now… you know say you can tell me anything.' Noga said.

'Na dis man Mustapha' Muna began.

'Mustapha, Mustapha … Na who he be?'Noga said

'Come on my friend, no take me play!' Muna-Muna barked.

'Play? Play? Which kind play I go take you play?' Noga said

'I say no take me play O! You know say my brain dey hot, no be small boy like you wey go just dribble me anyhow....' Muna said, looking insulted.

'Me I no know about dribble o, but I just want tell you say I no know any Mustapha' Noga insisted.

'Okay... okay, if na so you want am... you no bin know say I am a C.I.D. yes I am even in S.S.S, I am a top Security Officer na because I lie to you say I don retire for police… Okay na you find trouble, Akintola Noga e don tey since we been dey watch you… you and that

Mustapha we get hot informations about una.' He stood up knocking over the empty beer bottles in his contrived anger.

'Oh yes na for tribunal we go talk am, na for de panel hand you go remember this Mustapha wey you talk say you no know.' He began to walk away, he had played his ace and every step he took was now a step away from Mustapha his quarry. It worked; Akintola Noga couldn't risk the fact that he may not have been telling the truth.

'Muna …Muna!' he said out loud 'Muna-Muna!'

Muna-Muna turned.

'Okay come, please come, you know say I no fit deny everything from my friend. Please come help me, that Mustapha forced me. He forced me he is a dangerous man, a very dangerous man. I need help and protection from the Criminal Investigation Department from the State Security Services. I beg you come and help me!' he said there was fear in his voice.

Muna-Muna returned, feigning reluctance, but in his mind he smiled, a first victory. He would find out all that he knew and maybe even force Noga to help him.

They talked for a little while as Madame Calabar's beer parlor filled up with the frustrated poor who drank away their sorrows. Muna continued his bluff. He made up stories, many hideous crimes that Mustapha committed and told him that the Security Organization was ready to eliminate Mustapha. He convinced him that there was only one way in which he, Noga, could save his own skin. He could only avoid the tribunal and firing squad by helping the State. That would mean assisting the undercover agent, who was Muna-Muna himself, on the elimination exercise. Akintola Noga was afraid. He knew about so called 'justice' and he had often seen septic police cells and heard well-founded rumors of the torture; being 'hung' upside down for hours the pliers and the teeth, the metal wire up the Urethra. He didn't want any of that on his precious sexual equipment; he was prepared to jump into a lifeboat to avoid the sinking ship. So he held onto Muna-Muna as much as possible and tried to use him to save himself. He had been had.

THIRTY-TWO

THURSDAY 5ᵀᴴ MARCH 1985

I

Flight 501: from Lagos to London. Akin relaxed a little, the most difficult part had passed. He had successfully taken the briefcase from the fat customs officer and on to the aircraft. The cold air filtered slowly from the air-conditioning nozzles onto his sweating face. He tried to slow his heart, which, in spite of the tranquilizer, pulsated rapidly. He wiped his damp forehead with a handkerchief, asked for a soft drink as the D.C.10 aircraft slowly filled with passengers. He looked out to the tarmac; luggage being loaded into an aircraft opposite, taxiing planes, elephant grass in the distance. He tried to reassure himself that it would be alright, he had done it several times before. He looked down at the brown leather attaché case and his heart missed a beat. He fiddled with his rings and held on to the seat. '*Calm down*', he said speaking to himself between deep breaths, '*Calm down, now, easy, easy...*' And he felt better.

He closed his eyes and thought of life, sweet life. He thought of Binta, beautiful Binta. And he forced himself to dream a little. His mind conjured up the benefits of the last trip. He could see himself in places he had only heard of, Paris, New York, Acapulco and some sybaritic resorts in the Caribbean. He could envision Binta with him. He would take her wherever she wanted. They would be happy together; making love every day, swimming in the blue ocean, dancing beneath the stars and dining at the very best places. This would be the last time, the very last he reminded himself. He looked down at his feet and smiled to himself. He had walked the razor's edge several times.

The captain welcomed the passengers on board as the turbojets whined. The orders were given to cabin staff to close the doors. The pressurized cabin was cool compared to the hot yellow day that burnt outside. He could feel the aircraft roll a little and he felt a little relieved. He smiled to himself as they taxied. '*Hell*' said under his breath '*Acapulco here I 'come!*' Romano would really have to respect him after this one. As he knew that in the case there was up to a million dollars in uncut cocaine hydrochloride. He asked for some scotch to celebrate the success of the first hurdle. The hostess brought him a double with ice and he gulped it, his hand still shaking as he emptied the glass and placed it on the table. He set his head back, closed his eyes and tried to sleep.

II

In the cockpit the captain received a message from the control tower that the aircraft was not to take off. He was asked to wait at the end of the runway and was told that it was not required that the flight should be delayed too long.

A combat green camouflage military Land Rover sped down the runway to the aircraft; it was followed by several others and with the mobile stairs in tow. When they reached the idling plane, soldiers jumped down from the Land Rovers armed with sub-machine guns with sickle-shaped magazines in their hands and encircled the aircraft and pointed their guns at the pilot. The heat raged and via the radio the control tower instructed him to switch off and open the doors. This he did. Outside an officer descended from the green Land Rover closest to the aircraft. He wore dark sunglasses, his combat uniform, also camouflage green, was starched and ironed to crisp perfection. He walked, on gleaming black polished boots that dazzled in the sunlight with his revolver in his hands.

Meanwhile, Akin thought of Binta, of how he would hug her and hold her when he returned from England triumphant. He was surprised but not worried when the captain announced that there were little delays from the control tower and technical issues with the aircraft and as such he would have to open the doors. He opened his eyes as he felt the thick humid heat enter the cabin. His heart sank when he saw the familiar face of Major Musa Ahmed as he entered the cabin. He realized that the game was up. That he had been done in and that he would possibly never see Binta ever again.

THIRTY-THREE

FRIDAY 31ˢᵀ MAY 1985

A meeting had been secretly arranged, no one knew anything about it, not a whisper, and it was absolutely secret. It was afternoon and Mustapha was away to a meeting with some potential runners for new shipments of cocaine. He was also to meet with an Indian who promised to supply him with large shipments of heroin. Romano perspired in the warm afternoon as he walked quickly on a small road between two houses that led to a beer parlor in Surulere. He skipped over an open gutter full of stagnant water. He spat and cursed under his breath, for having to make his living in this wretched country. He hated the smell, the weather, the heat and the itchy life. But it was so alive, he acknowledged, there was so much that was animal about it.

The taxi horns tooted about him and he heard voices all around him. As he walked he put his hand into his jacket and felt for his pistol. The message he had received hadn't told him whom he was to meet. From his experience meetings like this always spelt trouble. He was prepared, the tingling sensation of awareness flowed through him making him ready for action. He approached the dark bungalow and entered.

His sight failed temporarily, for a split second, on account of the change of light. He held his pistol tighter, his finger on the trigger ready for anything. His nostrils were filled with the smell of beer, palm wine, and spicy African food. He walked around the bar, his shoes scrunching on the sand of the concrete floor, until a man waved a handkerchief at him. That was the signal. Romano walked cautiously towards him. He realized that at this point it was impossible not to take a risk, he would never go down alone, and he would shoot the man in the corner as well.

'Sit,' the man invited.

Romano sat down still holding fervently onto his pistol.

'Musa sent me' he said 'I am to give you a number and details.'

Romano scribbled down a number which the man gave him and they ordered a beer which they split, one glass for each of them, as a sign of good intentions. But there was little good in their discussions. The radio played highlife music and Romano surveyed the squalid drinking parlor and wondered what sort of people came to such places. He had not expected that the meeting could change his life. The effect of what he had planned had not sunk in. The man stood, stretched out his hand and shook him.

'Make it look like an accident,' he said. 'Pick the right moment, and when he's dead not only will the money be waiting for you... There will be much more.'

Romano stood out amid the brown faces. As he walked away, perspiration beading on his temples, he remembered a line from a film he had seen once, a film about a Scottish King; '*I go and it is done, the bell invites me, hear it not... for it is a knell that summons thee to heaven or to hell.*'

THIRTY-FOUR

FRIDAY 31ST MAY 1985

I

Akintola Noga sat in Madame Calabar's waiting for Muna-Muna. He did not ask for a beer or any other drink as he was not at all thirsty. It was a hot day and the flies that inhabited the fetid environment fed on spilled beer and palm wine. He tried unsuccessfully to swat a couple of them with his handkerchief. But he was too slow.

'Our big madam! I beg you come wipe this table, now, na so, so fly wey plenty here!' he said slightly agitated. For the past three weeks he had been unable to sleep peacefully and had stayed up alert thinking about his life. The cause of his insomnia was fear. Muna-Muna's threats had shaken him and he had on several occasions attempted to tell his guardian and boss Mustapha, of the threats from the old policeman. But his cowardice and selfishness had got the better of him. He was prepared to attempt to save himself and throw Mustapha to the dogs. He wore a tired and dejected expression as he looked up at Muna who had just walked in from the afternoon heat.

'Noga? Wetin dey worry you abi you dey sick? See as your eye red and your hand dey shake na malaria?' Muna asked.

'No no be malaria, I just tire well, well.' He settled down opposite him.

'Madame, bring us beer I beg' Muna ordered.

'No beer for me' Noga said resisting the offer.

'Take small of my own e go clear the sickness for your body.' Noga had to agree to a glass of beer, there was no resisting Muna. Between his thoughts and his fears and his plans of how he would save himself he wondered how Muna-Muna managed to stay alive considering the quantity of beer he drank all the time.

'Na for brewery them go bury you when you die,' Noga said, feigning humor.

'Yes I go like that one well well... so that for night I go commit for my grave begin knack endless beer' Muna said smiling and showing off his teeth.

They discussed Muna-Muna's plans. But Muna did not tell him everything. He asked for a description of Mustapha's house in Victoria Island and he drew this with a pencil on a page of his drawing book. He asked about the neighbors, about the security, Romano's abilities. Muna was meticulous in his preparations. He asked Noga if he could drive and they arranged to borrow a Peugeot 504 from the Customs Department. A large 'tip' to the official driver and the security on duty at the offices in the evening would secure the car for one night. He even made arrangements for the local electricity department to leave one of their ladders used for inspecting overhead cables to be near Mustapha's house to make scaling the wall easier for him.

'Old boy you must help me o!' Noga implored.

'Make you no worry at all, you dey my hand.' Muna said, reassuring him

'I beg, you know say na una get us for this country, help me from this man, help me please!'

His voice was filled with the fear that was written on his face, in his eyes and etched deep in his heart. And Muna patted his hands and held them in his two hands.

'Ah...ah na wetin? I dey here' he said assuring him.

Muna-Muna did not tell him the exact day on which they would go and get Mustapha but he told him that it would be within the next few weeks.

And they left separately, the sun burning their dark brown skins. Muna to Mushin, Akintola Noga to Ikeja. Muna's blood boiled, the fight that he had nurtured in the pit of his stomach thickened and it consumed him, his vengeful passion had solidified to steely courage. He was prepared to battle with the mighty.

II

SATURDAY 1ST JUNE 1985

'Dis na traditional place!' The man in a loincloth said abruptly as he stood, challenging him, legs apart blocking the sandy white path that led to a small hut behind the large grey rock.

'Eh heh now, na traditional place wey me I dey find' Muna said.

'Who send you come find am?' he questioned aggressively. 'I say … who bin send you come find our traditional place!' he persisted. His eyes were red, a sure sign of the liberal use of the local moonshine known as *kai-kai*.

'Na my wife people... them, them…' Muna said stammering.

'Them been talk say make I come this place make my body come strong well, wells' he continued. The man relaxed a little and looked at him.

'Na where your wife from come?' he asked Muna.

'Na from Bala here... Just Bala here' Muna replied smiling foolishly.

'Okay,' the man said holding a small *calabash* towards him.

'Na wetin you go take open de road... na only twenty naira fit open de road for person wey no be son of our soil.', He said and Muna reached into the pocket of his trousers, brought out a twenty Naira note, and dropped it into the calabash. The man smiled. He was a short muscular man, bare-chested and he wore no shoes with a little red cap on his head. Muna-Muna walked behind him. Every ten meters or so, the man would stop. Spit to his right and left, mumble some words under his breath and continue.

Muna had risen with the sun. He travelled early in a taxi, a lightning speed Peugeot station wagon and the driver, who had been high on kola nuts and other secret potions and drinks, had pushed the car beyond the manufacturer's speed limits. He had travelled through Ibadan, Ogbomosho and towards the town of Ilorin and had turned left off the road before Ilorin towards the small town of Bala. The taxi had dropped him on the road to Bala and he had walked for one kilometer until he reached the tall tree in a grove that marked the entrance to the shrine. They entered the thatch roofed hut that leaned on the rock, it was dark and cool inside. The man turned to him and mumbled some more incantations.

'You must *commot* your trouser and shirt O! for this place we no dey allow anything wey *Onyibo* dey wear… *commot* de watch too.' Muna quickly removed all his apparel and the man handed him a small loincloth which hardly covered his big stomach.

'Now you don reach our traditional place, make you *siddon* here', he instructed Muna and pointed to a low stool for him to sit. Muna sat.

'Na wetin you want make our ancestors do for you?... Na money you want or you want make annoder person die?' the man asked him

'No be una go kill am for me, na me go kill am!' Muna said.

'Na him I dey ask you now? …Na wetin you want?' he asked again forcefully.

'I want make you make am say bullet no go enter my body!' Muna said.

'Make bullet no enter your body, eh... that one na small thing' he said.

'Take this seven days *palmy* first wash your blood make all the dirty wey *Onyibo* don put for your body commot.' he instructed as he handed him some pungent palm wine in an open gourd.

Muna drank the stale palm wine. He would have preferred beer and he was just about to ask the man if he had any beer when it occurred to him that beer too was a white man's creation and as such, his request might annoy the guardian of the shrine. He had faith in the little man and his dirty old palm wine, the *traditional place* and what was due to come. He would gladly come here every day and not go to a church. It never occurred to him that those who came with the church had taken over his land. He emptied the gourd and burped.

'Before our ancestors go hear you, you must open them ear well… well!' the man said pushing the calabash towards him for more money. Muna reached for his trousers and brought out another twenty Naira note.

'No be twenty naira O! *Haba!* Na forty Naira wey go open the ear of our ancestors.' The man commanded with finality. He reluctantly put another twenty naira in the calabash.

'Lie down here now!' the man said and Muna-Muna lay on the smooth mud floor, his stomach sticking up like a large mound of earth. The man picked up some white chalk and spread it on him. He mumbled some more incoherent stuff. He walked out and brought a small, fluffy chick which he killed by twisting its small neck. He slit the little bird's throat with a rusty razor blade and spread the fresh blood on Muna. Then he sipped some stale palm wine. All the while, Muna lay, eyes closed, allowing his body to be covered in blood and white chalk dust. There were chirps from birds that drifted into the shrine as the yellow sun shone gently. It was a fine day.

Finally, the guardian of the shrine broke two eggs on his chest and mixed it in with the blood and chalk. He was absolutely covered in muck.

'Make you no follow woman otherwise bullet go tear your belle!' he warned and Muna wondered what he would tell his wife when it was cold at night.

After a few more smelly drinks, Muna-Muna dressed and left. He had to 'close the road' with another twenty Naira. He felt safe and he believed that now Mustapha's bullets would not penetrate his skin. He walked, under the hot afternoon sun, to the junction and waited there for a taxi or a bus to come by.

THIRTY-FIVE

14TH JUNE 1985

The air, cool and fresh, blew through her hair. Binta sat with Mustapha in the Fletcher speedboat. The outboard engines churned the water from deep blue to white suds as it propelled them forwards. Sea water sprayed on her face, as she looked out from behind dark sunglasses to the buildings on Queens Drive and Eleke Crescent. It was late afternoon and a little cool. They were on their way to Mustapha's beach house in Tarkwa Bay. They went down Five Cowries Creek, under the bridge that separated Lagos Island from Victoria Island, past the Yacht Club, down the harbor channel towards Tarkwa Bay and Lighthouse Beach. Mustapha said nothing as he pushed the outboards, Mercury Black Max's, to their limits.

They could have gone by helicopter but Mustapha had not used his boat in a long while. So he instructed Rob Bungham and Romano to come for him the next morning in the chopper. As they approached the Takwa Jetty, Binta thought of Muna-Muna and Akintola Noga, she wondered how they were getting on. She felt a little worried for Muna-Muna as she had, in spite of his boorishness, come to like him. It may not have been unconnected with the fact that he was Akin's uncle. She didn't want any harm to come to him at all, at least on her account. At the same time though, she wanted Mustapha to have a taste his own medicine. Why should he be free and alive when Akin was dead, almost shot by Mustapha himself? She thought. She had thought several times of getting him by herself but she lacked the guts. She was not a killer.

'Just you and me this weekend...'Mustapha said as he slowed the boat down, its nose dropping and the hull bouncing, splashes on fiberglass, as the waves rocked her. Binta was silent and she gazed at the empty beach.

They walked down the jetty, Mustapha carrying the bags in one hand, the other over her shoulder.

'Just you and me this weekend' he said once more.

'Nice, it feels so serene,' she said lying.

They both lied to each other. The love had gone and it was all a veneer of pretense and make-believe theatrics while the truth of dark and vengeful bitterness lurked in their treacherous hearts. They walked to a split level building with large bay windows upstairs and glass sliding doors in front. Binta walked in and Mustapha went round the back to look in the shed. It was there that he kept his dirt bike. An evening sea breeze fanned over the island as day came slowly to an end; he knew what he had to do. But he would wait until the right time.

THIRTY SIX

Tuesday 9ᵗʰ April 1985

I

Akin could no longer distinguish between night and day because of his erratic sleeping habits in the dark cell. But his impending death hung over him. He knew his execution was near. Like an animal awaiting slaughter, he stared into the darkness. He was now a shadow of his former self; dark bags beneath his tired eyes, his skin, now almost an ashy grey had lost its healthy cocoa brown sheen and he had lost much weight, as he sat dejected in Kirikiri Prison.

Dying, the fear of the living was never easy. Especially for Akin who had made such a profound effort to live, to enjoy life. The fear of death, the cold hand that would obliterate his sweet life, was compounded by the torture of his incarceration. The repugnant smell of human excreta and urine that hung in the almost septic prison contributed to the total subjugation of his once youthful spirit. With nostalgic longing he thought, of times past, the sweet, almost effortless days of the boom. Of the time he had made quick money from Mustapha, of Binta; her soft smooth skin, her warm embrace, it was beauty lost. He had, throughout the trial by the tribunal, dismissed his romance with her as contrived and mawkish. But now, as he walked the plank of his execution, the shark-infested waters about to receive him, he tried to hold onto whatever pleasant memories that he possessed. They were all that remained.

Memories, he felt a tear as it trickled down his face, he had shed many in his solitude as he cried himself to sleep. He awoke, still thinking of Binta; had she been or had she not been? He asked himself. His life, his struggle, came to him in flashes, the sweet more often than the bitter. He remembered how she had taken to him, not entirely innocently, but without that aloof reserve that the noveau riche so often have in Lagos. His heart had gone out to her, on account of her humility, for he realized, through and through, that she belonged to a different status of birth. He sat there, his head swelling with admiration for her and he cried again, a broken man.

They brought him food, insipid beans, and dirty water and he shoveled it, out of hunger, into his mouth, swallowing forcefully, so as not to taste the mish mash. In the darkness he could see his only friends, the cockroaches crawling in and out of the cracks in the cement floor and there were mosquitoes that sang in his ear and sucked some of his little remaining blood. He had grown accustomed to mosquitoes and his entire skin had become a pincushion for proboscis' but to him the physical torture was little, for it was his soul that really concerned him. He wondered about his soul, his spirit, for he stood on the precipice, staring into the abyss of afterlife.

The doctor had been, declaring him, as a veterinarian would an animal, fit for slaughter, for execution, fit to be killed. He wondered if there was a need to be fit to die and it seemed totally senseless to him. But so did being killed for carrying a briefcase with cocaine in it. He was everything but fit. He was hardly a man, even a shadow of a man. He was crouched now, his own pungent odors even repelling to himself, reduced by fear of the end, the inevitable end, to a sweating, shivering, coward. He was alone in his cell, a privilege of the death sentence. He had previously been in a cell with nine others who had also been condemned to death for cocaine trafficking and they had fought. It was on that account that he had the stitches on his forehead; a septic wound which had been seen by some kind prison warden who had recommended penicillin powder and careless ugly stitches. What did it matter any way, if a dead man had stitches or a wound?

He thought about himself; before he met Binta what had he been? He wondered. And to that he felt small, he had been nothing and had become nothing. But what is love worth in a world like this? He wondered. He had wizened in his misery, his grim insignificance, and to him it was all philosophy. Why her? Why me? Why was I born the way I was born? Why here? Why now? And his unanswered questions further frustrated him. He felt like smashing his head into the wall or doing something equally self damaging. Instead he slept, tumbling into his misery infested id as his world, reality, crumbled about him.

II

The metal clang of the opening lock and the large bolt sliding stiffly awoke him. There was some light from the corridor. A warden walked in with an officer behind him.

'Akin Muna?' the officer said crisply.

'Yes' Akin replied weakly.

'You are to come with us' he instructed. But Akin could not move. He was frozen by weakness. The officer leaned into the corridor

'You there... He called to a warden seated at the end. 'Come and carry him to bath!'

And two wardens held him, one on either side, and led him into the light towards the washing facilities. His eyes hurt as his pupils contracted, not having seen any light lately. He was bathed for the first time in more than two weeks with cheap key soap. The cool fresh water tumbled through his bushy hair and washed him slowly, revitalizing him as water does, and he felt stronger, cleaner, back to the living world.

After he had been bathed they dressed him in some clean clothes that had been brought by a girl. He asked them what girl but they refused to tell him. And he hoped that it was Binta, at least he would have the comfort of believing that she had been faithful to the end. He was taken to a small room with dirty white walls; it was an office of some sort on account of the desks and old dusty files that lay carelessly placed all over the room. He was seated on a wooden bench and his eyes darted about, betraying his nervousness, searching the room. There was a light that hung beneath the sagging cardboard ceiling boards on which the candle-smoke-stained cream gloss paint peeled in parts indicating that in the day time it was a hot and humid room. There was an open window with a chicken wire grill across it. He could see the pale light of dawn outside and he wondered how much longer there could be for him. He felt beads of sweat as they trickled cold down his back.

'Na wetin you want chop?' the warden asked. Akin thought for a while and replied, 'rice and dodo.'

'You want smoke?' the warden said thrusting a packet of Three Rings cigarettes towards him. Akin hesitated a little and took one, it had been a while since he had last smoked and he missed his cigarillos. The warden struck a match and he lit his cigarette. He smoked nervously inhaling the smoke more rapidly than he usually would and he felt little benefit. His mind went to God, the protector of his soul. He had never been religious and only during his short stay at his aunt's house had he been to church once or twice. In his fear, he became a gambler, willing to stake his soul for salvation. He knew no conventional prayers so as he sat in the little office smoking three rings cigarettes he said a prayer which he made up as he went along;

'Please God he said under his breath. I know I'm a dirty man, please, please, please help me... I know that they say you will take the poor and the needy into your house so take me... Please take me!' As an afterthought he added 'God please, please look after Binta so that no harm should befall her when I am gone.' he felt better, a little better, but somewhere in his skeptical human soul he wondered if there was a God with a house for the poor and needy. His rice and dodo came and he ate. Between his prayer and meal dawn had come lighting the day, a day that he was sure would be his death day.

III

He was tied to a stake along with the others and like a player on the stage he could not see the crowds, the sun rose and the heat came and he could hear the men, women, children, beggars all about him. The cameras were clicking and the nation and the world were soon to have some more blood to smear on already blood-caked hands. He could hear the screams of people above the murmuring: 'cocaine waya o!', 'Poor man no get brother', '...Na him cause am.' but most clear was the shout from a man whom he could scarcely make out, a man who was dressed in a white *aladura* habit 'the wages of sin is deaths!..., Is deaths!' and at hearing this he froze, the time had come he thought. The soldiers, starched automatons, took their positions ready to shoot. And he became incontinent, his body no longer in his control, surplus adrenalin pumping through his system, warm wet urine staining his clean trousers trickled down to his feet and he was dead from fear before the bullets hit him. His body which was full of hormones, jerked fitfully as his flesh was torn by bullets. He died a dirty death on Wednesday, the 10th of April, 1985. And none would care but Binta.

THIRTY SEVEN

Evening, the blue sky was slowly engulfed by darkness as the sun, a disappearing orange arc, set on the horizon. Binta looked at the receding day, towards the beach and the Atlantic. As she stood by the open window, the ocean's breath, a warm sea breeze, blew gently through her hair. She felt it, nature caressing her. As she dressed, freshly scrubbed and her beauty glowing radiantly, she had a feeling in her heart, her female intuition irked her, she was convinced that he now knew of everything; Akin, her pregnancy and that she was no longer in love with him. She would have to pretend, make it very good for they would be together for the whole weekend.

Downstairs, Mustapha sat in front of the marble coffee table on which he had set up his free basing equipment; a specially designed copper wok with a small burner beneath it. He placed his unloaded pistol beside the burner and switched it on. The metal heated quickly and the cocaine hydrochloride gave up its fumes. He moved his face over it and inhaled, breathing in deeply as he was propelled into tranquility. Binta came down, smiling falsely and walked to the kitchen.

'Come here,' he said.

'I'll just get myself a soft drink' she said

'Come on have a little.' He said

'No, I really don't feel like it,' she said.

'Come on! Let's have a wild weekend' Mustapha said inhaling some more. He stood, swaying a little and walked towards her. She could see the bulge in his crotch. It was always like that when he was high.

Mustapha held her, 'come on baby,' he said squeezing her. He lit a coca paste laced rolie and held her hair roughly caressing it.

'Why?' he asked 'why don't you want to enjoy yourself?' She hated his touch and moved away.

'You don't like my hands but I like your hair' he said roughly pulling her to him. He moved quickly and she could feel the steely strength in his fingers as he pulled her to the fumes, held her arm behind her and forced her to inhale.

'I said take a breath!' he said agitated.

Reluctantly she took in the fumes and she could feel the ache in her head as it seemed to explode. He touched her breasts and felt her nipples harden. She no longer resisted and inhaled of her own accord. Mustapha handed the remainder of the rolie to her and walked to the kitchen.

'Let's have some champagne' he said.

She puffed what remained of the stub, almost burning her lips. She could feel the warmth that began at the pit of her stomach and spread through her legs, a tingling sensation. She was again enslaved to the chemical that left her body aching for seduction; in her mind she imagined his body.

They drank the cold wine greedily, wanting to get it down, out of the way. 'This is more like it' Mustapha said as he moved closer to her and held her. She melted at his touch. He kissed her, her face her ears she moaned at his touch. They writhed as he freed himself, hurriedly undressed her and entered her warm snugness quickly. She twisted, dry and unprepared, but he held her midriff lifting her from the sofa and slammed into her in a piston-like motion. She began making an animal mewing noise. He held her hard, riveted to her, and she felt the pleasure, and as she came she twitched and called his name. He turned her over and continued as he had lost his sensitivity. She shivered, coming several times before he spent himself. As they lay satiated she could hear in the background the deep rumble of breaking waves on the beach, and the sea breeze that whistled through the open windows. She lay on the sofa, the room spinning around her; she was unable to stay awake. Mustapha got up walked upstairs and returned shortly with a silver vial which held cocaine, with the aid of a little spoon he sniffed some, snorting sharply. She watched him through half open eyes as he filled himself with the potent drug. He was preparing himself for the act. Somewhere in his twisted heart he knew that he loved her, as much as he could love anyone. He refused to accept that he still felt that way. He couldn't accept the truth. To him it was all a lie, a charade. He thought of the photographs and his imagination ran amok. He could see them together, their bodies intertwined in fornication. And he felt insulted, that his woman should use him, spread her legs for Akin. He burned with jealousy and he sort vengeance.

'Binta, Binta, Binta...' he said, his accent more African than ever, 'why? What was it that I didn't do for you? What didn't I give you? Why did you have to make a damn fool of me, of Mustapha?' he continued. She noticed his eyes, slightly bloodshot, as they twinkled with hate and she was petrified.

'I gave you the world, heaven on earth!' he screamed.

'No Mustie, no, you gave me nothing, what's the use of coke money when you're alone? damn you, you left me alone all the time... you think you can buy everything, life, people a country, but not love.., that's one thing you can't buy, love!'

'Shut up, you ungrateful bitch!' he spat.

'Why should I shut up? Why... you listen, listen to the damn truth, if everyone around you is afraid to talk I'm not!' She replied in a steely voice.

'The truth is that you're a damn whore... you don't think I know of Akin, of the little bastard that you have growing in your dirty womb' he said

'Look. Mustie, you think you know love, you don't know anything, you think just because you can buy hate, get killers to put someone away, that you're a man? You're nothing, not even a man because you're so spiteful. All you know is hate, evil, vengeance, all you are is made up of hate; it's in your blood!' she said

He didn't want to listen to her but it was forced on him, he thought that she was wrong, how could she know the truth? He asked himself. How could she ever know what she had meant and he would end it all, he stalked her, shaking with anger as she stumbled over the coffee table.

'Come here, Binta!' He barked.

She could see that he was beyond calling; in his murderous eyes she could see the danger of the man whom all feared. He smiled, lunged at her and held her hair, pulled her towards him and picked up his pistol. She shook, in fear like a dying deer, her breath quickening as he pushed the cold steel behind her neck. He moved it down between her legs.

'That's what you like eh come on this is what you like!' He said. He pointed the pistol to her head and squeezed the trigger. She fainted as the firing pin clicked sharply in the empty gun.

'Come on get up!' He said slapping her round the face. 'It's not time yet, not yet time for you to go!' He stood her up as tears trickled down her face. 'A few more seconds,' he said 'I'll give you a few more seconds to live... I am God!' he screamed in crazed blasphemy as he raised his clenched fist in a black power sign. 'I am God!' He shouted almost at the top of his voice. He had lost his mind to the potent chemicals in his bloodstream and he was gone…far, far away in a sea of madness. He swung round and hit her face with the side of the pistol. It cracked her tooth and cut her lip. Courage welled up inside her when she saw blood and she was ready to stand up and struggle for her life. She would never beg, not her, not beg a dirty little rat like Mustapha.

'You bastard!' she screamed and a voice in her head said *run, run, run*!

III

She flung the wok at him and ran out onto the beach. She could hardly see where she was going as tears filled her eyes. She ran aimlessly, a petrified animal. In the clear night air the moon glowed like a silver coin. She ran, stumbling in the sand of the beach as the world swirled about her. She was high on cocaine. She tried to slip off her shoes, her heart raced as she ran through the sand, panting. She was trembling as she heard the sound of the motorcycle speeding towards her. She turned in frenzy, wide eyed and afraid, looking for a place to hide as she fell, picked herself up again and continued towards the large rocks at the curve of the bay.

It all seemed dream-like, as if she were in a trance, soft and slow, each step she took seemed like a leap to her and she fell. It was all real. In fear her stomach felt vacant as though it floated outside her being and she lay there retching and then she vomited on the white sand. He rode her down. As she struggled to stand, he jumped off the motorcycle and held her. It took only a fraction of a second and finally she would be free of him as he held her head in a vice-like grip and snapped her neck with a sharp twist. He let her drop, and without another look from his glazed eyes, he left. The rain came down all at once in large droplets and washed Binta's corpse as the waves broke rhythmically on the beach.

Mustapha rode around the beach and then back to the house. There he found a paste-laced rolie and lay naked on the floor with it smoking between his lips. As he lay he could only think of Binta. Where was she? He asked himself, where has she gone? I'm sure she's here, he wondered. Maybe she ran off with Akin. No, she can't have. Akin's dead, I saw to that, yes. I sent her there, too. That's where she is; she's burning in hell with Akin!

'Farewell Binta Farewell!' he screamed and he laughed with a high pitched eerie cackle like a madman as he puffed on his rolie. The minutes slowed, the room faded out of vision, the world darkened and into the land of Morpheus he went, to sleep.

In the morning, Romano and Rob Bungham went to Tarkwa Bay in the helicopter. They found him unconscious on the floor. They saw her on the beach. Dug a hole nearby and unceremoniously buried her; desecrated her. Then they took Mustapha back to Victoria Island. As Bungham settled the helicopter on the rooftop helipad and switched off he was shivering. Romano carried Mustapha on his shoulder like a sack.

'Romano?' Bungham said 'what's going on. . I know I shouldn't ask, you know, see nothing hear nothing like the boss says but hell this is crazy! Jesus that woman …'He stuttered still trembling '... that woman, she was, she was one hell of a lady. Can you tell me? Can anyone tell me? What's going on here? Tell me, please, please!' He said pleading in bewildered disbelief. And he held Romano's hand as he bent double, sobbing, tears in his eyes.

'Never should have come here, never should have, this crazy country, this hell on earth. She didn't do any drugs did she... did she… please tell me Romano... tell me, I'm lost?' he continued.

Romano touched his hair lightly and squeezed his hand but said nothing. He walked away from the aircraft to the stairs Mustapha still over his shoulder. He wondered how it had all come to be, how the plot thickened with every passing day. Yesterday Binta, today no Binta.

He was still a thinking man even though the thoughts crept out of his mind at the oddest times. He realized that Mustapha was almost past it and that soon it would all be over. He would endeavor to protect himself at all times for no matter how loyal he was to Mustapha, it was important to look after one's own interests and ultimately, one's life. He cast his eyes over the blue haze of morning mist that hung over the waking city and shrouded the umbrella-like palm trees. The cool and fresh morning breeze blew gently over the house and across the Island and the city as God breathed on mankind.

THIRTY-EIGHT

17th JUNE 1985- 8PM

I

Musa Ahmed stood, the sea breeze fanning him, on the balcony of his hotel suite. He was a little tired at the end of the day, having had to walk up fifteen flights of stairs several times at the office on account of the power failure. He felt blue, a little lonely, and living in a hotel didn't help much. He thought about the past and about the future and he felt a little sad that the plans for the coup d'état had been altered. He had been to Switzerland several times and had paid bribes to his neighbor, the officer whose orders were to keep him under surveillance. It was true that the arrangements had been changed. But nothing was ever plain sailing; he would pay money and spread the cash around as he had not revealed to them all of the funds Mustapha had given him, there was still a lot in reserve to buy his way out and quell the opposition that had reared its head. He would also promise lucrative and powerful positions to his peers, who were always prepared to take a chance, back a dark horse and ride on it to power. They believed it was unwise to step on the neck of a possible head of state. He swigged brandy, smooth Remy Martin, and walked around the room, unhappy. He thought of many things and not only of power. And he no longer felt beaten, a little weak and vulnerable. In his mind he was back in charge of things, dictating the outcome of the future.

When the setbacks to the plans had come he had been a little dejected, he had always had ambition as his reason for existence and for that short period before he believed he was able to sort things out in his melancholy he questioned ambition. He thought about his son, the fifteen year old in America and wondered what he would do if he became Head of State. He felt like picking up the telephone and placing a call to the Military School, but he changed his mind. He wondered, about the whole military idea and whether it was right to make his son a second generation officer. There was a knock on the door, but he was not startled as he had been expecting his dinner to come. He walked up to the door, with his pistol in his belt and peeped through it at the steward outside. He let him in and soon settled to his dinner. But he was not hungry, so he pecked at his rice and chicken and had several brandies.

It was late and he was tired. As he undressed, he realized that he would have to bring the date forward, so as to contain the leakage and opposition. He would have to make it soon, he wouldn't tell Mustapha. He changed into pink silk pajamas, put his loaded Browning as usual into the drawer in his bedside table and settled, placing his head on the soft down cushion, ready to sleep. As he tumbled easily to sleep, on account of the brandy, his mind pondered constantly the big decision as to the timing, the decision that would mean his and the life and death of many men. He had on his shoulders, as he slept, the burden of kings, as he thought about his future and his actions which would affect the destiny of millions.

II

An evening sea breeze filled the room as he slept. A man crept in quietly like the air itself and floated towards his bed. He opened his eyes; alert as always and in the deep blue of darkness he thought that he had seen the shape of a man. Still groggy, he reached for his pistol. As his hand entered the drawer, it was slammed; the man kicked it shut on his wrist. He screamed and struggled to free his trapped hand. The man held his wrist; his boots pressed down Musa's arm, on the edge of the bedside table and brought the machete swiftly down on his metacarpals. Musa screamed in excruciating pain, as his hand was left hanging. He tried to think, confused in agony, he rolled, falling off the bed hitting the lamp switch accidentally. The room was flooded with light and he recognized his assailant as the intelligence officer who had been in his room. He could not think any more. The hard military boot hit him in the face and Musa heard his nose break as the man kicked him. He kicked him again in the face, this time, breaking his front teeth. He could taste blood and saliva as it filled his mouth and dribbled onto the carpet. Inside him, his will told him to fight back. There was little fight left in him and if he had been able to speak he would plead on his knees for his life. There were several kicks to the stomach, groin and ribs and the machete cut into his thighs spilling blood as he was butchered further. He coughed more blood. The man picked him up swiftly and stood him. He twisted his semi-severed right wrist and dropped the hand as it was ripped off. There was more blood. He held Musa's neck from behind his head, twisted an arm behind his body and smashed his face into the wall. Musa felt no more pain, saw no more light; he slid slowly into darkness as he died. The man laid Musa's mutilated body on the bed, took two steps backwards and saluted his corpse crisply, in a show of demented military etiquette. Musa would never be Head of State. As he left the room, he dropped the machete and removed his black leather gloves.

THIRTY NINE

9.30PM MONDAY 17TH JUNE, 1985

Mustapha was in bed and he tried to read a detective novel in order to force his alert mind to sleep. In the next room Romano set up playing cards. He played patience on the night watch and he placed his revolver beside him on the table.

A green Peugeot saloon pulled up about a hundred meters from the gate of the house and a man got out. Muna-Muna was dressed in black as he walked nimbly from the car towards the gate. Noga turned the car round and waited in it as the engine idled. They had bribed the operators in electricity authority to ensure that the power supply in the area was to be switched off at 9.35 and he waited, impatiently looking at his watch for the blackout. It would take at least a minute for Mustapha's automatic standby generator to kick to life and that would be enough for Muna to creep into the house and stop the lights coming back on.

At 9.37pm the arranged power cut happened and Muna-Muna climbed over the gate, with the aid of the pre arranged ladder, past the inactive infra red alarm sensors. He went into the open garage where Akintola Noga had described to him the position of the electricity panel. While there, he switched off the generator switch, so that when the automatic generator switched on there would still be no electrical current flowing from the generator into the house. Stealthily, Muna-Muna picked the lock of the garage door and entered into the house through the kitchen.

Upstairs Mustapha shouted in darkness.

'Romano!' He yelled

'Yes, yes the generator should be on,' Romano replied, groping in the dark.'

'Then check it, I want to read!' He ordered.

'I can hear it, the generator's on so there must be a fault somewhere' Romano said.

'Then check all the switches' Mustapha said.

Romano picked up his revolver and made his way downstairs. Muna-Muna had crept into the sitting room and he was crouched behind a sofa. He heard the voices and as his eyes adjusted to the darkness he could see the spiral staircase and the figure of Romano as he descended. Muna-Muna waited for the figure to pass by him and go through the kitchen door. Romano walked through the garage to check first the switch in the generator house.

'Hey hurry up, what's all this!' Mustapha screamed.

Muna went quickly up the stairs and into the room from which Mustapha's voice had come. It was dark there but he could make out the shape of a man.

'Romano, is that you? Where is the light?' Mustapha said.

Muna-Muna took a shot; a sharp crack into the room the sound travelled far in the still night air. Romano heard it and fiddled with the switch downstairs. Muna-Muna quickly went back to his hiding place behind the sofa. The lights came on as Romano threw on the generator light switch. 'Damn' Romano muttered as he rushed into the house, his mind alert and adrenalin pumping through his system. Like a tiger he was ready to spring as he crawled stealthily round the corners, his revolver nozzle always going first ready to spit .45 slugs. He went into Mustapha's bedroom; the blue sheets were stained red with fresh arterial blood. Mustapha held his right leg but he was still alive.

'There's a man in here! I want him under now, dead, iced...move now!' he said.

Romano attempted to advance to examine Mustapha's wounds.

'Move I'll take care of myself!' Mustapha barked.

Muna on hearing the voices ran out of the house through the kitchen and into the garage. Before he left he pulled the generator switch plunging the building into darkness once more. Romano followed; labored by darkness he bumped into the coffee table and tripped over the rug in the sitting room. Muna ran to the gate, climbed it and entered the car as Noga pulled away screeching and raising dust and gravel on the road. They sped off. Romano, down and outside the garage was only able to see the red tail lights about to turn the corner at the end of the road. He cursed and knew that the only way he would catch up with them was if he took the Harley Davidson, he leapt on it, started up and the motorcycle growled to life, he clicked the electric gates open and followed in rapid murderous pursuit. Soon the air was blowing through his hair and he held his pistol in his right hand as he chased after them. In the speeding Peugeot Muna-Muna screamed at Noga.

'My friend will you move this car... You no see say the man dey come!' He said, his voice trembling.

He leaned out of the window and shot twice at the fast approaching man on the motorcycle, his shots missed entirely. Romano, usually the tiger in any fight, was relaxed as the night air blew through his open shirt. He took a shot at the tires of the car. Rising in a puff, asphalt and dust indicated where his off target bullet had hit the road. He had hoped to stop the car and then finish off the occupants but a better idea occurred to him.

He smiled as he aimed for the petrol tank and took a shot at the car which was not less than fifty meters away. The tank exploded as he made a direct hit and the burning car careened and hit a concrete electricity pillar. Romano took several shots to make certain that there would be no survivors and then geared down, replaced his revolver and spun the bike in an effortless 360 degree turn. It was too easy, he thought, much too easy. Then he breathed in deeply a few times and sped back to his boss. He was not concerned about the identity of the men in the car; it didn't matter, as they were dead. Soon the news would spread like wildfire through the underworld organizations that it was still impossible to hit Mustapha.

'It's all fixed:' Romano said as he walked into Mustapha's bedroom. The bleeding man lay in agony.

'Call me the Doc' he said groaning in pain.

Mustapha did not expect it. Romano stepped back, raised his pistol and pulled the trigger. The bullet grazed his neck and he was transfixed, frozen in shock as he stared at his bodyguard. Romano squeezed again, a bullet straight to the head, instant death. There would be no more farewells, no more fast deals, fast women and easy kills. Instead he would face the final judgment before God; he was now on his way to Hades where he would surely twist eternally in scorching and consuming hellfire as his soul paid the price for murder, for his wretched life.

Romano put down his gun, hardly looking at the bloodstained bed. He walked downstairs to the telephone. 'Hello is that the Police? I want to report an armed robbery at…' the incident would remain one of the many unsolved and brutal armed robbery cases that were frequent in the wild city. He sat on the chaise, and from the cigar box on the coffee table took and lit his first coca paste laced rolie. He smoked, the smoke soothed him and he wandered into the realms of tranquility. He thought about all that had passed; of Akin and the note that he had sent him. He had quite liked Akin. He thought of the future and from his newly acquired position of power, he made plans of what he was to do with the power and money. It was now his outfit; Romano Moreno's Organization.

THE END

Printed in Great Britain
by Amazon